Alexandra David-Néel

Alexandra David-Néel

Portrait of an Adventurer

RUTH MIDDLETON

SHAMBHALA
Boston & Shaftesbury
1989

Shambhala Publications, Inc.
Horticultural Hall
300 Massachusetts Avenue
Boston, Massachusetts 02115

Shambhala Publications, Inc.
The Old School House
The Courtyard, Bell Street
Shaftesbury, Dorset SP7 8BP
England

9 8 7 6 5 4 3 2 1

First Edition

Printed in the United States of America

Distributed in the United States by Random House
and in Canada by Random House of Canada Ltd.

Distributed in the United Kingdom by Element Books Ltd.

The photographs are reproduced with the permission of the
Archives-Fondation Alexandra David-Néel, Digne, France,
with the exception of the photograph of Samten Dzong,
which was taken by Ruth Middleton.

Library of Congress Cataloging-in-Publication Data
Middleton, Ruth.
Alexandra David-Neel: portrait of an adventurer/Ruth Middleton.
p.   cm.   Bibliography: p.   Includes index.   ISBN 0-87773-413-5
1. David-Neel, Alexandra, 1868–1969.   2. Scholars, Buddhist—
France—Biography.   I. Title.
BQ950.A937M53   1989
294.3'092'4—dc19   88-34337
[B]   CIP

To Palmer, Cindy, and Veronica

Contents

Preface

I arrived as the potatoes were burning. The kitchen window was flung open, and a strange voice demanded the reason for my presence at this inconvenient hour. In France one arrives at noon only if invited. When I replied that I had an appointment with Mlle. Peyronnet, the voice was joined by a smiling face. "You must be her American friend. Do come in." Even after seven years in France, my accent is still a dead giveaway. From the trunk of my small Peugeot, I removed the flowers and fruit I had brought as my offering to the household of Alexandra David-Néel, and mounted the steep incline leading to the entrance of the home she had christened Samten Dzong, which in Tibetan means "Fortress of Meditation."

It was the secretary, Frank, who opened the door, and I sensed a deep fatigue behind the warmth of his smile. Inside all was confusion. The "Fortress of Meditation" had been invaded by a group of well-meaning but overly persistent women who were determined to purchase the dining-room table out from under the very luncheon they were delaying. "Marie-Ma" Peyronnet was doing her best to persuade them that this was impossible. Frank led me to the kitchen, where I was formally introduced to an American friend, Helene Carter, who had greeted me from the window. We began to fuss with the obstreperous pressure-cooker, while Frank took charge of the flowers. The noise in the dining room seemed to subside as the problem of the table resolved itself, only to be succeeded by the sound of a beautiful Tibetan bell, with which Marie-Ma signaled to the resident Tibetan *geshe*, Ngawang Khenrab-lags, that he should descend to the dining room. When he arrived she told him that she had bartered for it and was thrilled with her acquisition, which had a lovely silver tone. Would it be (she hoped) an acceptable addition to the altar in the *salle de meditation?* The geshe smiled. It was very nice, but perhaps not the "bargain" she had imagined. At this point, Frank's French appetite overcame his Buddhist restraint. It was half past the hour. "We are here to eat, not to discuss commercial ventures. *A table!*" Laughing, we arranged ourselves around the rescued table. The geshe at the head, wearing the traditional garnet robe, presided over this bizarre collection of people of diverse ages and origins. The youthful (and hungry) Frank is secretary to Marie-Ma, who served as Alexandra's secretary during the last ten years of her life, and who has maintained Samten Dzong as a museum and cultural center since the death of Alexandra in 1969. Algerian by birth, she is connected to some secret source of energy that never fails to impress me. Her explosive vitality is matched only by her sincerity and warmth. To my left, Helene, French by birth, American by marriage, provided the necessary glue that kept the conversation from flying apart. Finally, there was myself, an American painter living in France. But of course there was also Alexandra, whose presence still dominates Samten Dzong, though her ashes joined the current of the Ganges over fifteen years ago. It was she, in truth, who had brought us together over this luncheon.

Our conversation centered on the recent visit of His Holiness, the Dalai Lama, who had just departed after five days in the city of Digne. He had come, not as a ruler in exile, but as a simple Buddhist monk. His mission was to share with an enormous gathering of Europeans and exiled compatriots, now living in Switzerland and France, the doctrine that has been emerging from Communist-occupied Tibet and Dharamsala, India. Each successive day that he had appeared in the

Palais des Congrès, seated on his traditional throne and surrounded by an entourage of lamas, the audience had increased. Wherever he circulated, whether on foot or by automobile, a growing number of people gathered, magnetized by his presence, hoping to receive the comfort of his blessing, or to be rewarded by even a brief glimpse of his radiant smile. The resonance of his hearty laughter echoed still among us.

A rich mixture of impressions assaulted my senses in this small room where past and present were being fused. Incense and burned potatoes, ringing bells and ringing laughter, the blending of varied accents in animated conversation, punctuated by Marie-Ma's "Servez-vous, servez-vous." "More potatoes, even if they are scorched!" filled Alexandra's "fortress."

When it first was that I heard of her, I cannot truthfully say. My own interest in Buddhism goes back to my awakening enthusiasm for the art of the Far East in the early 1940s. I recall quite vividly a sensation of deep regret (possibly as I read her obituary) that this woman for whom I felt such a strong affinity had disappeared without my having had the opportunity to meet her. Little did I anticipate the future! Two years after I had installed myself in a small village in Provence, I discovered how close I was to her former home. It was the publicity announcing the first visit of His Holiness in 1982 that brought it to my attention, and resulted in my undertaking the first of many *promenades* across the undulating landscape that lies between my home and Digne. During this period my command of French, forced by my constructing a house in a region where no one spoke English, had developed to a level where Mme. Néel's books, many of which have never been translated into English, were at last accessible to me. As I pored over the pages, I became aware that my coming to France was in truth a migration of greater consequence than I had imagined. On winter nights I closed my shutters against the starlit chill of Provence, and entered the world of Alexandra. Through the long hours, wrapped in shawls against the cold as my unattended fire was reduced to embers, I became increasingly fascinated and involved. I joined her pilgrimages through India, China, Japan, Mongolia, and Tibet. I allowed her to guide me through the mazes of mystery and magic that lured her incessantly into unexplored regions. I witnessed her awakening to the wisdom of Buddhist teaching, laughed over the asides inspired by British colonial protocol, and marveled at the determination with which she availed herself of her minuscule bathtub, undaunted by the rigors of the Himalayan winter. By day, on canvas, I explored the landscape of southern France. By night I climbed the Himalayan peaks and traversed the Chinese deserts. Inevitably my two words began to merge, the inner and outer landscapes to harmonize.

I began to visualize Alexandra, to create in my mind a portrait of this woman who so intrigued me, and for whom I had developed a great admiration. After repeated conversations with Marie-Ma I decided to realize this "portrait" in written form. It was of particular importance to me because Alexandra had such great affection for the United States. In the diary in which she noted the events of each day, as well as her most personal observations, she wrote: "Very early I felt an attraction for America—for an America 'dreamed' . . . and at that time if it would have been possible, I would have wished to become an American by adoption."

In a way I would be carrying out her wish. Without the devoted assistance of Marie-Ma this project would never have achieved its present dimensions. During the long winter months I remained in Digne, she made available to me all the unpublished material in the Archives at Samten Dzong. These included the complete letters (published and unpublished) addressed to Alexandra's husband, Philippe Néel, her daily engagement diaries, boxes of letters received from all over the world (from Gandhi, Arnaud Desjardins, Mira Alfassa, Gaston

Doumergue, president of France, Elizabeth, queen of Belgium, Christmas Humphreys, Evans-Wentz, et cetera, et cetera), numerous unpublished manuscripts, and drawers filled with hundreds of carefully filed photographs, most of them taken by Alexandra herself. Perhaps most important of all were the daily conversations "over the teacups" with Marie-Ma, and the taped interviews to which she graciously consented. Marie-Ma recounted innumerable anecdotes about her years with Alexandra, sharing observations of those who were close to her and those who came to visit. She shared with me the stories of her childhood and youth that Alexandra had repeated in her old age. These were undoubtedly augmented and embellished after many repetitions, but nevertheless they preserved much of the flavor of the European bourgeois world in which Alexandra developed and against which she rebelled. I was privileged to spend countless hours at Samten Dzong, immersing myself in the world Alexandra had created there.

The very fact that one has chosen to tell the story of another's life implies a subjective approach. When one begins to examine the material that has been amassed over a period of one hundred years, selection becomes imperative. Since the author has also lived, experienced, and responded over a period of time, the choices can be made in that context and no other. What unfolds under these conditions is, in effect, a dialogue. Picasso was one of those who recognized this process and built it into a system of discovery. But it does not cease there. The painting, so the artist hopes, will be observed, the book read, the music absorbed. And the listener, the observer, the reader, the third participant is forced also to respond out of the envelope of consciousness in which he has been formed. We see what is there for us. We absorb what we are willing to let in.

This is the history of an encounter. My hope is to make it come alive to a degree that those who read it will

participate in the conversation, and will share the enthusiasm that makes of living a true adventure.

Ruth Middleton
Venasque, France, 1987

Acknowledgments

I wish to mention those people whose helpful encouragement contributed so much to this undertaking. The greatest support came from Marie-Madeleine Peyronnet, who devoted hours during her busy schedule to making the unpublished material and photographs included in this book available to me. I am deeply grateful to Emily Hilburn Sell for staying with the project in spite of a pressing (and much more important) commitment. Appreciation is also due those who read, corrected, and made helpful comments concerning the manuscript, especially Caroline Birdsall, Alice Stewart, Sarah Hall, Veronica Kleeman, Shannon Gilligan, Ray Montgomery, and Eleanor Cheney. Without the patient technical assistance of Alan Miner, John Kleeman, and the entire staff of Val-Com, the work might well have lived (and died) within the memory of my word processor. My thanks to all of you.

Introduction

A portrait, whether of an apple, a flower, or a woman, exists against a background. Since my self-appointed task is to create a portrait of Alexandra David-Néel, this background must first be established and "brushed in," however freely. There are actually two planes: the middle ground, which, very appropriately, I will identify as Buddhism, the religion, the philosophy, the field of research and study, and the far distance, composed of the historical facts of the century from 1868 to 1969. It is in the context of these two interacting "grounds" that Alexandra played out the drama of her life.

When she was born in 1868, the crinolines of the Empress Eugénie and her court were still in style. When she died in 1969, the "hourglass," the bustle, the *tailleur anglais*, the redingote, the sheath, and the miniskirt had seen their day and been discarded. She herself, during her travels in the Orient, wore slacks that would have horrified her mother. Alexandra, who first observed the delights of the Champs-Elysées from a horse-drawn carriage, and who assaulted the Himalayas mounted on a yak, lived to be the proud possessor of an automobile and to travel in an airplane. As she evolved beyond the social and political limitations of her nineteenth-century girlhood, she even went so far as to abandon (before it was The Mode) that basic item of feminine apparel—the corset! The marriages of properly reared young French women in the nineteenth and early twentieth century were arranged, not in heaven, but in the office of a *notaire*, between two sets of practical parents whose interests were entirely material. Alexandra, refusing to be subjected to this ritual, was, for a time, partner in a free relationship, and ultimately decided for herself whom she would marry.

The life of the French Third Republic, which replaced the empire of Napoleon III in 1871, is well known to Americans because their wealthy compatriots developed, in the early twentieth century, an enthusiasm for the French painters known as impressionists. *La Belle Epoque*, as the period between 1871 and 1914 is known, fills the canvases of Manet, Monet, Renoir, and Degas that confront the visitor to any major American museum. The attitude expected of the young women glorified by Renoir and Manet is well defined by contemporary historian Alain Decaux in his monumental *Histoire des Françaises*. He quotes Genevieve Gennari, writing in 1895: "Train your daughters to sacrifice their favorite occupations, if need be, to be available to entertain their brothers, without showing, of course, that they would prefer to be doing something else."[1]

For the bourgeoise, only two things were of real importance: the family and the home. This all-consuming interest in domesticity was made possible in part by the presence (in 1906) of 760,000 women domestics in France. Servants were considered not a luxury but a necessity, and all but the most impoverished managed to find someone to serve them.[2]

The other major concern of Renoir's ladies was *la mode*, an obsession inherited from their mothers and grandmothers of the second empire. The fabric shops owned by Alexandra's mother flourished because *la mode* required yards and yards of elegant satins, velvets, and expensive Belgian lace. The old farmhouses of the region of Provence where I now live still bear traces of the vanished silk industry of southern France. Increasing imports from the Orient ultimately caused the decline of this industry, and brought other influences that would be important in Alexandra's life. Alexandra's descriptions of her mother always emphasize the fact that she was attired in yards of lace, and her own "presentation" gown was a marvel of the couturier's art, white brocade covered lavishly with lace. In the portraits painted by the French impressionists the emphasis is often on transparent fichus revealing delicious white shoulders, brocade bodices enclosing minuscule waists, and wide velvet skirts supported by any number of lace petticoats, of which an occasional discreet glimpse is offered. The "foundation" of this magnificent architecture of style was, quite literally, the famous French corset that forced the female body, regardless of any amount of suffering, into the shape of the current fashions. It required the assistance of one, if not two, of the above-mentioned domestics during the twenty-plus minutes required for lacing. Alain Decaux mentions, in an amusing aside, that the Paris lost-objects bureau was the final repository of hundreds of these creations, abandoned in carriages by elegant ladies rushing home after an amorous rendez-vous had detained them a little too long.[3]

" 'La Belle Epoque': thirty years of peace, the ladies of Maxims, the tra-la-la of polkas, the cozy atmosphere of intimate little dinners, the newspaper for a penny, profits at three percent. . . . *Quo Vadis* appeared, and a bronze statue of Victor Hugo was installed. 'La Belle Epoque'? Or the Ugly? A society that seemed to exist with its eyes firmly closed against the suffering of the world."[4]

Although the majority of the middle class paid lip service to the Church, the lower classes, both in the city and, with a few exceptions, in the country, had long since been de-Christianized by the misery they suffered. The lack of concern for their condition shown by the Church caused them to turn away. Behind the scenes, a rebellion was quietly forming, whose manifestations began, timidly at first, to appear. And this rebellion was in large part due to the activities of certain intrepid women. In 1892, when Marie Curie arrived in Paris to pursue her studies, the benches of the Sorbonne were no longer exclusively reserved for men. Among the working classes, brave young women were struggling against great odds to improve the conditions of their underpaid, overworked sisters. Gradually the sentiments of these women began to be expressed, even in the elegant salons of such grandes dames as Mme. Menard-Dorian and Mme. Arman de Caillavet, where Anatole France, enthroned in an armchair, held an entire generation spellbound with his stories. It should be stressed that these "bourgeois socialists" were interested only in promulgating theories. Under no circumstances would they have considered associating with the underprivileged people whose condition they deplored. But at least there was the beginning of awareness.

And Buddhism? Why Buddhism? Many of my French contemporaries, granddaughters of La Belle Epoque, ask me this question. What attracted Alexandra David-Néel to the teachings of Shakyamuni Buddha? The Thirteenth Dalai Lama himself posed the question during their precedent-shattering interview in 1911.

The very excesses and paradoxes of La Belle Epoque caused many thinking people to examine themselves and the time in which they lived. Beneath the seeming frivolity of the period there were the beginnings of a conflict that would explode only after the artillery of the 1914–1918 war had been stilled.

Buddhism had begun to move west in the nineteenth century as it had moved east many centuries before, along the silk route (that same route that terminated in the boutiques of Alexandra's mother, Alexandrine David). Because the British were most vigorously engaged in trading with the Orient, it was among the English colonials that the first interest was born. Translations of Buddhist texts began to appear sporadically in the nineteenth century, and such translators as Max Müller and Rhys Davids made works available for the first time to Western scholars, while Sir Edwin Arnold's *Light of Asia* brought the story of the historical Buddha to popular attention. In 1891 an American, Colonel H. S. Alcott, founder of the Theosophical Society, prepared a list of fourteen "fundamental Buddhist beliefs" as a common platform, a kind of "Buddhist catechism" of all the Buddhist schools. When Alexandra was studying in London in 1888, many translations of Oriental texts were already available. But the first attempt to make Buddhism available as a philosophy to be lived rather than a subject for scholarly research was the founding in 1907 in London of the Buddhist Society of Great Britain and Ireland.[5]

The greatest if most subtle influence, however, was that of Buddhist objects of art. These arrived in profusion, collected by travelers in the Far East, to fill the museums and private collections of England and Europe during the nineteenth century. Even the paper, printed with popular illustrations, in which Japanese porcelains were wrapped became an object of study and decoration. The serenity expressed by the buddhas and bodhisattvas in meditation had an enormous appeal when introduced into the frenetic, materialistic atmosphere of contemporary society. The vast emptiness of Japanese and Chinese landscape painting offered a restful alternative to the crowded, overcharged "classical" landscapes favored by the academies.

Alexandra, intent on exploring all possible avenues of personal development, must have become aware of Buddhist teachings at the same time she was investigating the writings of the Latin philosophers and the Gnostics. She recorded her first introduction to Buddhist mythology at the age of thirteen, when she was a student in Brussels at the Convent of the Bois Fleuri. Her interest was most certainly nurtured during her period of study in London. Her increasing facility with English made the translated texts available to her. But she herself emphasized that the greatest influence was her contact with the oriental pieces in the Musée Guimet in Paris. As with so many Westerners, it was the visual image that precipitated an awakening to the philosophic content. Alexandra explained to the astonished Dalai Lama that she had become a Buddhist through a subsequent study of the literature. No teachers capable of transmitting the oral tradition were then available in France. Les Amis du Bouddhisme in Paris was not founded until 1929, by Constant Lounsbery, an American.

But the time was ripe for Eastern philosophy to appear in Europe. For over a century the glories of antiquity alone had been exalted. Early in her life Alexandra, like all European children, was introduced to the classics—to Latin texts, to the Stoics and especially to Epictetus. Classicism was everywhere in evidence, especially in architecture, painting, literature, and decoration. It was the foundation of all French education, public and private. The academies accepted only those works of art that were concerned with classical subjects, historical or mythological in content. Combined with this was a total adherence to Cartesian rationalism, proclaimed by Descartes. The dignity of man was seen to exist exclusively in his reason, in his faculties of analysis and criticism. The romantic movement, so important in Germany and England in the early nineteenth century, had never really taken root in France. A few of the paintings of Delacroix had been recognized, but with reservations. Sensitivity, spontaneity, and intuition were all suspect. (Women alone were allowed a certain degree of freedom in this regard!) The discoveries of Pasteur, Poincaré, Comte, and the Curies only fortified the French conviction that all progress in the future would be based on the exercise of reason served by scientific investigation.

Then, toward the end of the nineteenth century, a new movement began to be manifest. Influences from without were working on the intellectual and artistic life of France. These came from many directions: from Germany, in the writings of Hartmann, Schopenhauer, and

Nietzsche; from Russia, with Tolstoy and Dostoevsky; from Scandinavia, with Ibsen, Strindberg, and Swedenborg; and there were the strange romantic creations of the American Edgar Allan Poe, which created a sensation in literary circles. A wave of pessimism swept across France, leaving in its wake a revival of religious evangelism, Protestantism, agnosticism, mysticism and many nondogmatic beliefs. And it is not surprising that the "religions of human suffering," as some of these were called, opened the doors to the Orient. Courses in Orientology began to be offered by Professors Foucher, at the Sorbonne, and Sylvain Lévi at the Collège de France. Lecture halls filled and overflowed into the corridors. The lively discussions that ensued were continued in salons and cafés throughout Paris.

This "aesthetic spiritualism" resulted in a movement in arts and letters known as symbolism, the influence of which is still being felt. It totally rejected the positivist, rational point of view that had dominated intellectual activity since Descartes. It brought with it a nostalgia for the past, especially for the Middle Ages, for Gothic expression in architecture, music, and literature, and spawned a multitude of works by such writers as Mallarmé, Verlaine, Maeterlinck, Claudel, and Bergson. It was fortified by a general loss of confidence in the value of scientific progress on the one hand and, on the other, by the discoveries of Charcot, Bernheim, Janet, and Freud, which revealed the hitherto unexplored depths of the subconscious mind. Suddenly, thinking men and women were confronted with questions that had outrageous implications for the future, with an ambiguity and paradox that could be surmounted only by some process of transcendence. For the painters and musicians this became possible through the creation of new and hitherto unimagined images and tonalities. For the intellectuals it would require abandoning the safe ground on which they had stood for centuries. On the benches of the Sorbonne, in the salons and cafés, young people like

Alexandra David were suddenly exposed to a cataclysm of ideas that would sweep away the safe, secure nineteenth-century world into which they had been born.

Gradually the voluptuous contours of Renoir's ladies dissolved in the sunlight that caressed the water lilies in Monet's garden. Sunflowers were literally exploding across the canvases of Van Gogh. The visible world had assumed the form of dancing particles implied by Indian sages long before the Christian era. William Butler Yeats predicted that the center would not hold. And beneath the golden Buddha in the Musée Guimet, Alexandra David plotted an itinerary that would conduct her through the mazes of the occult. In her survival kit she included the counsel of Ecclesiastes, the maxims of Epictetus, the *Bhagavad Gita,* and the intuitive understanding that true wisdom is to be found within. "Let truth be your torch and your refuge and seek no other."[6] Most important, she always retained her French skepticism and her keen sense of humor.

The miles she traversed can be plotted with accuracy on the maps of Europe, North Africa, and Asia. Her interior pilgrimage from Freemasonry, French Protestantism, and intellectual rebellion, through the overpopulated worlds of music, theater, journalism, arts, and letters, to the solitary pursuit of Hindu and Buddhist teachings is more complicated. When did the dispassionate and objective student merge with those subjects she had considered merely a field of observation? With admirable candor she described the loneliness, nostalgia, and depression that interfered with her intellectual detachment. She freely admitted her repugnance for the filth and discomfort she was forced to endure, and managed, in spite of incredible obstacles, to indulge in her daily bath, trundling a small zinc bathtub across the wastes and jungles she explored. She never ceased to be a civilized Parisienne. But the openness of her mind knew no limits. The eminent French theologian and philosopher Teilhard de Chardin, seated beside her at a dinner party, observed, "Madame, I assume you do not believe in miracles." To which she replied, with a mischievous smile, "But of course, Father, I perform them all the time!"[7]

1

A Small Anarchist

«1868~1886»

The situation would have been comic, had it not been for the gravity of the very young child, who stubbornly refused to identify herself to the *gendarme* towering above her. She stood quietly before him, her small hands pressed defiantly together. The guardian of the Bois de Vincennes was beside himself with anger and frustration.

What could he possibly do to save face before this minuscule demon? He had at first congratulated himself on rescuing the little creature, seemingly lost among the towering trees of the park. Her elegant costume and her carefully arranged curls tied with assorted ribbons identified her as the daughter of wealthy parents. He was already dreaming of a substantial reward, which augmented steadily as the situation became more and more humiliating. He had not counted on the firmness of her resolution, nor the sharpness of her fingernails. She seemed not in the least frightened, only resentful that her exploration had been interrupted. Her small pointed chin was thrust out, and she maintained a silence that was shocking in a little girl. Little girls were supposed to cry with fear, or sob with relief. But her comportment bore little resemblance to the way little girls were supposed to behave in the year 1873 in an elegant suburb of Paris.

His rescue suddenly appeared in the form of a fellow gendarme accompanied, not by distraught parents, but by a soberly dressed governess who stood beside him, clenching and unclenching the handle of an expensive parasol. "Alexandra, where have you been?"

With extreme dignity, the child replied, "I was exploring the *bois*, searching for my very own tree." The tone of voice implied that this was the most normal of pursuits for a spring afternoon. The governess, obviously accustomed to replies of this nature, paid the guardian generously for his trouble and removed the source of his chagrin. The leitmotif of the long adventure of Alexandra David's life had been composed: "Alexandra, where have you been?"[1] The child who sought her "very own tree" with such passion would continue to pursue her own way with unparalleled persistence, to penetrate Eastern mysteries that no other Western woman would dare, and in the process would create her own legend. How did such an "original" emerge?

Her father, Louis David, had been born in the city of Tours in 1815, a nephew of the famous French portrait painter David. Early in his academic career he developed into a brilliant student. As he pursued his education he began to show promise as a man of letters. For a number of years he tried teaching, but eventually turned his considerable talent to journalism and politics, becoming director of the *Courier de l'Indre-et-Loire*. Rigorously Protestant, he was a Huguenot by confession, a committed socialist and Freemason, bitterly opposed to the monarchy of Louis Philippe. His strong republican sympathies drew him to participate in the Revolution of 1848. After the accession of Napoleon III, he was forced to exile himself in Belgium with his good friend and corevolutionary, Victor Hugo.

There, he met Alexandrine Borghmans, whom he married in 1854. She was the twenty-three-year-old daughter of a wealthy and socially prominent family. Theirs was the very model of a satisfactory bourgeois marriage of the time, a bulwark of respectability, a calculated merging of interests. But her mentality stood in dramatic contrast to that of her husband. She was a devout Roman Catholic and a loyal supporter of the Belgian monarchy. She was a most unusual mixture of Dutch, Norwegian, and Siberian ancestry. But in spite of this colorful inheritance, Alexandrine was a perfect example of complacent self-satisfaction, whose primary interest was the profit she derived from her many investments. Alexandra described her mother as a large woman enveloped in lace, resting her ample contours on piles of pillows, devouring not only quantities of delicious Belgian chocolates, but one popular adventure story after another.

Louis David had made it clear that he did not want children. Alexandrine, on the other hand, had dreamed for years of being the mother of a son who would one day become a bishop of the Roman Catholic Church to which she was so devoted. At the age of thirty-six, after thirteen years of marriage, her will finally prevailed.

Savoring her triumph, Alexandrine whiled away the months of her pregnancy absorbed in the novels of James Fenimore Cooper. Thus, while Alexandra formed within her, she traversed the swamps and forests in the company of Leatherstocking, always supplied with chocolates and fluffy pillows. When, on October 24, 1868, the doctor announced to her that she was the mother of a fine, strong, baby girl, Alexandrine reacted by throwing herself against her mountain of lace-covered pillows, sobbing with rage and disappointment. She turned the unwanted child over to a series of nurses and governesses, abdicating any further responsibility for her care. Alexandra never forgave her mother. At the age of thirty-five she wrote to her husband that while he had played and been happy as a child, as was fitting for his age, she had had nothing but her pride, which served as a refuge.[2]

Because he wished his child to be born on French soil, Louis David had taken advantage of an amnesty for all political exiles, and returned to France. In 1867, the Davids settled in the gracious Parisian suburb of Saint-

Mandé, where Alexandra was born. She early established herself as a miniature anarchist, and developed to
a high degree the art of escaping. For the time being, her
parents' successful investments provided the means for
her to indulge her desires.

Her life in Paris was not without distractions. At the
Champs-Elysées, where she was taken by her governess,
her favorite amusement was the traditional performance
of marionettes that has delighted generations of young
Parisians. She identified so completely with poor Pier-
rot, always under attack from the vicious Guignol, that
one day she lost control and stormed the fragile theater
to rescue her favorite. Joined enthusiastically by the
other excited children, she put an end to the performance by bringing down the house—quite literally.

Her curiosity was insatiable. "How did that pointed
stone tree grow on the Place de la Concorde?" During
the frequent promenades she was allowed to make in the
company of a long succession of governesses, she noted
every detail with interest and excitement. Hopping with
agility from a carriage, she would pause to "tip" the
horse with a piece of sugar, and was off on another
adventure. Soon she was galloping away in a goat cart.
Escape! Escape! Her one overriding ambition had been
formed. She would boast as an old woman, "I learned to
run before I could walk."

The year 1871 was disastrous for France. The monarchy of Napoleon III had crumbled and been replaced by
a diffident Third Republic, which was forced to conclude
a humiliating treaty with Prussia. The treaty cost France
the infinite riches of Alsace and Lorraine and laid the
foundations for a greater conflict in 1914. In the vacuum
created by this period of transition there arose in Paris
a feeble government, cut off from the provinces and out
of touch with the sympathies of the rest of the country.
This government, considered insurgent by the official
government of the Third Republic, mounted a rebellion.
On March eighteenth, the army of the republic, which

had been removed to Versailles, moved against and successfully repressed the rebellion. But it was a bloody affair, and the "wall of the federals" in the cemetery Père Lachaise became a symbol of martyrdom for the Left that would mark the history of this period. Alexandra would never forget this experience of the Paris years. She was carried on the shoulders of her republican father to see where the insurgents had just been executed. Many years later she wrote her husband about the day she was taken to the walls of the Federals when the cadavers were being hastily piled in the trenches that had been dug. Alexandra was two years old at the time.[3]

The father who had not wanted a child had decided to take her in charge. From the beginning she was trained to stare life and death unflinchingly in the face. David even began to include her on his frequent hunting expeditions. Although the sight of the little bloodstained animals and birds filled her with disgust, she loved the companionship with her father, the picnic that was an important ritual, and the occasions provided for her to wander in the forest. It was at this time that she began to formulate an image of God as a tree. She felt her true friends to be the grass, the sunlight, the clouds. It was in these that life truly flowed, and one who could see and feel this need never feel alone. "I owe to these things the joy I would never have known otherwise," she wrote.[4]

In 1873 Mme. David gave birth to the longed-for boy child. But the would-be bishop was very fragile, and lived only a few months. His arrival, so joyfully celebrated, underscored for the five-year-old Alexandra her mother's rejection of her own small person. Watching the toilet of the baby with hostile curiosity, she was immediately repelled by the small appendage that dangled between his legs. She later attributed to this experience the beginning of her abhorrence for all things masculine.

By 1874 Mme. David, bored and still mourning the traumatic loss of her six-month-old son, persuaded her husband that they should return to Brussels, where she would have the consolation and comfort of her socially prominent family. Her daughter could be properly reared and presented at court. This prospect cannot have pleased Louis, the avowed antimonarchist, but he assented. Although his political inclinations were revolutionary, his domestic attitude called for the tranquillity that would allow him to pursue his own interests. Brussels would offer him the distractions he enjoyed.

Alexandra had already developed an obsession with the large atlas in the Davids' library. Belgium was so very small compared with other possibilities, such as India or China, but she accepted the change with stoic indifference. Shortly after the move from Paris to Brussels, Alexandra made an important decision. She abandoned the Catholic religion of her mother for the Protestant faith of her father. She was beginning to appreciate the fine art of revenge. A fascination with comparative religion was firmly established by her sixth year. And as it turned out, this interest, amounting to obsession, developed within the very walls of a Catholic convent in Brussels. Alexandra's formal education had begun in a very proper Calvinist boarding school. Although it had been her choice, the austerity of the setting resulted in sagging spirits and a falling off of her normally robust appetite to such a degree that the family physician was consulted. He recommended the more relaxed atmosphere of the Convent of the Bois Fleuri. She responded at once to the change of ambience as well as to the improved cuisine. She recovered her lost appetite, and began to thrive both physically and intellectually. She was one of five Protestant students accepted in the convent. Two were English, one was American, and one German. Since they were not required to attend the daily mass, they strolled in the garden and discussed religious questions. There were endless discussions among the young "heretics," as Alexandra called them, on the subject of the Holy Trinity. For Alexandra, it was simple. The same person, when engaged in different activities, was called by different names: doctor, hunter, reader, violinist, gardener, et cetera. "When God speaks," she said to an older girl, "He is the Word." "And the Holy Spirit?" inquired the American, a Unitarian. "That is when He thinks," replied Alexandra with confidence.[5] The good sisters were either unaware of the speculations thriving within their very cloisters, or were unusually liberal in their approach to educating young women. Perhaps they considered the girls' fall from grace to be so irrevocable as to be unworthy of their attention. At any rate no effort was made to remold the opinions of the young Protestant students. Alexandra cherished her memories of the Bois Fleuri throughout her life. It was for her a period of true awakening, when she was free to extend her curiosity in all directions.

The decor of her bedroom revealed her increasing preoccupation with comparative religion. Before a Chinese porcelain Buddha, a light always burned. Over her bed hung the figure of a Christ, and a large Bible occupied the place of honor on her table. Each night before retiring she read several verses.

Her avenues of escape were many. A capable reader by the age of four, she early discovered Jules Verne, and avidly explored the world in his company, aided by the enormous atlas that she perused every evening after the long-suffering governess had brushed her abundant curls and dressed her in the voluminous folds of a lace-trimmed nightgown. She had also discovered music. From the age of five she showed herself to be an accomplished pianist, and spent hours absorbed in an ever-expanding repertoire. Since she found the childish games of her contemporaries insufferably boring, she populated her hours of solitude with an exciting cast of personalities, who proved to be her most devoted companions. Her library expanded, and the melodies of Mozart, Schubert, and Schumann filled the air of the somber Brussels mansion.

As she matured she was rewarded by increasing atten-

tion from her father. He sought her out as an interesting
companion, far more stimulating than her complacent
mother, and they were often to be seen, hand in hand,
strolling along the boulevards and through the museums
of Brussels. Their discussions of history, religion, politics, and literature were long and absorbing. So involved
were they in their very special complicity, that the hours
passed unheeded, and winter evenings overtook them far
from home. When they returned to the house, however,
a pall of silence fell.

But these were not unhappy years. She made friends
at the convent among the older girls, and continued her
religious exploration with a study of the Gnostics. She
acquainted herself with the theories of the Swedish sci-
entist-theologian Emanuel Swedenborg. At one time it
was her belief that she was the reincarnation of a theologian who was being punished by rebirth as a woman.[6]
At the convent she was awarded so many prizes for her
academic excellence that even her mother was impressed
and made her a gift of a beautiful Japanese inkstand.
She completed the ensemble with an elegant pen, her
very first important purchase when she was considered
old enough to receive an allowance.

It was when she was thirteen that she heard for the
first time the legend of the supreme sacrifice of the
Buddha, according to which he offered his own body to
nourish a tigress that was about to die of starvation. She
found it the most beautiful story she had ever heard. It
was also while at the Bois Fleuri that she formulated her
life-long motto, taken from a phrase in Ecclesiastes:
"Walk in the ways of thine heart and in the sight of thine
eyes."

There is only one photograph that shows Alexandra
as a young child. In it a pretty little girl, elegantly
dressed (her mother did not neglect her wardrobe),
wears a serious, determined expression. But there is
another "portrait" in the archives of Digne that is even
more accurate and revealing. While studying at the Bois

Fleuri, Alexandra did a drawing of a house. The house is small, enclosed in a garden surrounded by a high wall. The roof is decorated by delicately carved oriental designs. Each tile is meticulously executed. What is most striking is the fact that the windows and the single door are firmly closed. They do not even possess handles. A catlike beast guards the closed door. The wall surrounding the courtyard, the contours of which are not softened by a single shrub or flower, is high and constructed of heavy stones. In the background stands a single, beautifully rendered tree. Tall and firmly planted, it stretches its protective branches as though in benediction over this austere scene. On close examination, however, one discovers an opening in the wall that gives onto the road, without a gate of any kind. Alexandra has made her escape. She is en route, following the destiny that will beckon for a century and beyond.

2

En Route

«1886~1893»

Mme. David was beginning to relax and enjoy the evening. The presentation had gone far better than she had hoped. Alexandra was ravishing. The white lace dress became her slender figure well, and the "reverence" she had made before the king and queen, rehearsed during weeks of preparation, had been perfection itself in its elegant grace. The good sisters of the Bois Fleuri deserved to be congratulated. One never knew about Alexandra, but after all these months of worry, of wondering whether, at the last minute, some caprice would cause her to refuse the presentation altogether, it had been a complete success. Alexandra was a daughter of whom one could be proud—at last.

For the poor woman there had been many moments of despair in recent years. Alexandra had for a time been lured by a former governess to the convent of the Carmelites. For weeks she went daily to pray and meditate in their chapel. When the governess herself had become a novice, Alexandra went to visit her. Happily, because she was so young (and the sisters hoped, impressionable) she was allowed inside the cloister to be with her friend for a brief period. Alexandra had imagined that the nuns indulged in various mysterious rites behind the dark curtains separating them from the congregation in the chapel, that they achieved transcendent heights of spirituality during long hours of prayer and meditation.

"She discovered that the Carmelites in no way resembled the conception she had after seeing representations of pale virgins in the stained-glass windows of ancient cathedrals.[1] The reality behind the curtained grill was a group of hard-working Flemish girls, with rosy cheeks, who spent much of their time cultivating cabbages in the convent garden. She never returned.

Then, there were the escapades, first to Holland and England, then to the Italian lakes. A telegram had finally arrived: "Come get me. Am without money." From the point of view of the *haute bourgeoisie* of that period, no more scandalous behavior could have been imagined. She had departed with only her raincoat and the maxims of Epictetus as baggage, wearing a false wedding ring so she would appear older than her sixteen years, had crossed the St. Gotthard Pass on foot, and had stayed alone in an Italian hotel. In the circle of her parents' friends there would be absolutely no chance of arranging a suitable marriage after such a shocking departure from conventional behavior. Fortunately it had been possible to keep the adventure a secret. No one knew—at least no one who mattered. But the *coup de grâce* had been her bland suggestion, during the long return by train to Brussels, that she would like to study medicine. A doctor! Who would have imagined such an idea? Of course her mother had made it clear at once that this was absolutely out of the question, that she had her own plans for Alexandra. If a career she must have, managing one of her mother's fabric concessions could be arranged. Her father's recent investments had been nothing short of disastrous. As an adult, unmarried daughter, Alexandra would be expected to begin adding her share to the family resources.

The presentation ball was drawing to a close. Young couples, flushed and exuberant after hours of waltzing, were beginning to drift from the dance floor and greet the waiting chaperones. But where was Alexandra? Her mother began to be uneasy as the crowd thinned and there was no sign of her. She finally made known her

increasing anxiety and several young men offered to
search among the deserted rooms and alcoves for her
missing daughter. Servants were summoned with torches
to illuminate the gardens. It was there at last that she
was discovered, beneath a tree, fast asleep. Curled in
the folds of her elegant ball gown, a small kitten had
joined her in slumber. It was a charming picture. But
the effect was lost on her poor, outraged mother. Once
again, Alexandra had triumphed. This time she had not
argued, complained, or rebelled overtly. She had simply
fallen asleep.

Not long after this event, in the same year of 1886,
Alexandra failed to appear for breakfast. A maid sent to
summon her returned with the brief comment, "Mademoiselle has left." But how? And for what destination?
This time she had been tempted by a more ambitious
voyage. Mounting her bicycle, she had started south.
Before returning she would have crossed the entire
length of France and discovered much of Spain. Arriving
home on her own this time, she had little to say about
what had taken place during the interval. She had left—
period. The punishment of this eighteen-year-old girl
was not an easy matter. Of what could she be deprived?
Her tastes were austere, her mode of life inspired by the
Stoics. She ate little, and had no interest in the distractions normal for her age. As for indulgences such as
clothes and jewelry, they had to be forced upon her. Her
parents shrugged their shoulders in resignation, a response that would become habitual.

In 1888 she made her second trip to London. She had
already made a brief trip to London in 1883, crossing by
a Channel ferry from a Dutch port where she and her
parents were spending a summer holiday. She had "wandered off" on her own and had returned without comment once her money was gone. We have, fortunately, a
detailed account of the second visit. It appears in the
first volume of memoirs published after her death, entitled *Le Sortilège du mystère*. A childhood friend travel-

ing in England had sent her a revue, published by an English occult society, covered in pale blue, with the intriguing title *Gnose supreme*. Alexandra received it as she was on her way to spend an afternoon in the Bois de la Cambre in Brussels.

It was a long time ago, but as an old woman she recalled the setting as clearly as if it were yesterday: the sun filtering through the leaves, decorating the lawn with alternating spots of light and shadow, herself, quite young, sitting on a bench, considering the revue that rested on her lap, and exclaiming in a soft voice, "These people are crazy!"[2]

She possessed, even at this young age, a critical intelligence that penetrated everything she observed. Nothing was refused her serious consideration, but nothing was accepted without first being carefully examined through the lens of reason. Of the Gnose Supreme she made the later comment that although at times she found such "extravagants" sympathetic, she never dreamed of taking them as models of behavior. She considered that beneath the aberration of the most absurd appearances there was a certain reality; but to discover it one was required to reflect carefully and investigate with precision.[3]

Long after her friend had returned from England Alexandra had continued to receive this and other periodicals of an esoteric nature from a certain Mrs. Morgan, a member of the Society of the Gnose Supreme with whom her friend had become acquainted. When Alexandra decided to improve her English with a period of study in England, she discovered through Mrs. Morgan that the members of the "Gnose" had a club in London that had several bedrooms for visitors. Mrs. Morgan arranged for Alexandra to stay there.

Arriving at Victoria Station late in the day, she expected to hire a cab to the club. But she had advanced only several steps on the platform when she was addressed by a tall young man who explained that Mrs.

Morgan had sent him to escort her. At the club, the vice-
president of the "Gnose" was waiting to receive her
personally. A large woman, she was dressed in a flowing
gray robe with long sleeves, decorated with the numerous
brooches and medals that signified her office. Alexandra
was shown to a vast bedroom, comfortably furnished,
the windows of which were covered by black shades. On
the wall hung a painting that seemed to depict an under-
water landscape with seashells, populated by angelic
creatures drifting in long robes. Too exhausted to pro-
long her examination of the bizarre decor, she soon fell
asleep.

Alexandra found the club pleasant and the other
members sympathetic but discreet. No one attempted to
proselytize. Alexandra appreciated the seclusion and felt
at the same time liberated. She spent long hours in the
library, which contained a large collection of translations of Chinese and Indian texts and other esoteric
subjects such as metaphysics, philosophy, astrology, and
alchemy. She discovered the infinite riches of the British
Museum. To find herself among people who did not
regard her interests as peculiar, and who allowed her to
explore at will, was an unaccustomed pleasure.

The only "mystical" incident she witnessed occurred
when a noninitiate entered the library, selected a book,
and unsuspectingly seated himself on a sofa where the
"astral" body of one of the instructors had chosen to
rest. (The initiates were aware that, from time to time,
their instructors, having attained higher levels of consciousness, chose to abandon their physical bodies and
make excursions here and there on the astral plane.)
The unsuspecting ignorant hastily departed, admonished
by the others in tones of shocked dismay. Those who
had recognized the astral form knelt reverently before
the sofa, but Alexandra admitted that she could see only
the usual swirls of mingled incense and tobacco smoke
that always filled the room.

She made a number of friends, among them Jacques

Villemain, a French painter who had spent some time in
England and Scotland, and whose symbolic landscapes
fascinated her. She noticed, however, that he was becoming increasingly withdrawn under the influence of the
Gnose. When he reappeared after what had been an
extended "retreat," Alexandra, in an attempt to distract
him from the depression he seemed to be suffering,
suggested a day's outing to visit the Crystal Palace, a
major London attraction. They boarded the train in a
dense fog and, lulled by the gentle motion, were soon
asleep. A sudden halt awakened them. Hours had
passed, and when Alexandra inquired for the Crystal
Palace, the astonished conductor told her that they were
well en route for Scotland! During their long wait for a
return train, Villemain recounted a number of strange
psychic experiences. He was convinced that this seeming
"accidental voyage" had brought them to the threshold
of a different reality. The heavy fog represented the
ephemeral barrier separating them from the "world
beyond" to which they had come very close. Alexandra
listened with a mixture of interest and skepticism. When
finally they regained London her first impulse was to
seek an Italian restaurant. She reflected more easily on
a full stomach. The following day she reached a decision.
Her command of English had greatly improved. She
decided the London experiment had delivered all she
could expect. The Crystal Palace would have to wait.
Throughout her entire life, she always knew when it was
time to move on. She departed for Paris.

Mrs. Morgan, whom she had seen from time to time,
had introduced her to other groups of seekers in London, including the Theosophical Society. This society
had been founded in New York in 1875 by an American,
Henry Steele Alcott, and a Russian, Helena Petrovna
Blavatsky. It had quickly assumed international stature,
however, and the main headquarters were situated in
India. The main objects of the society were to establish
a nucleus of universal human brotherhood, to promote

the study of comparative religion and philosophy, and to make a systematic study of occultism. Mme. Blavatsky (known as H.P.B.), claimed to have received an esoteric teaching from a number of Tibetan sages, with whom she was in communication through "channeling," as it is now known. This teaching she set forth in her books, *The Secret Doctrine, The Key to Theosophy, The Voice of the Silence*, and *Isis Unveiled*. When she died in 1891, she was succeeded as the society's leader by Annie Besant. The London center, which was of major importance, was luxuriously appointed. Alexandra very much enjoyed the evenings she spent there with Mrs. Morgan. When her friend learned of her intention to continue her studies in Paris, she offered to arrange accommodations for Alexandra in the Paris branch of the Theosophical Society.

She had pleasurable memories of the comfortably agreeable atmosphere of the London center, and the prospect of finding a similar situation in Paris was enchanting.[4]

Presenting herself at the address given her on the Boulevard St.-Michel, she had difficulty finding the Theosophists. She finally located their headquarters on the third floor of a commercial building, at the end of a long corridor. The door was opened by a tiny woman, "almost a midget," and Alexandra entered the antichamber with difficulty, pushing ahead of her the heavy valise she had carried up the long flight of stairs. The Paris headquarters of the Theosophists was such a far cry from their commodious London establishment that Alexandra inquired if indeed she was in the right place. M. Jourdan, a somewhat cadaverous individual who, it seemed, was the husband of the midget, assured her in solemn tones that it was indeed, and that Mlle. David was expected.

As the only "guest," she occupied a tiny, minimally furnished bedroom, directly off the dining room, which itself contained only a rude table and several straight chairs. When she asked where the bathroom was located, the astonished little woman informed her that a public bath was available on the same street, not too far away. As soon as Alexandra had arranged her belongings, "dinner" was announced. The meager furnishings of the dining room had caused Alexandra, by now very hungry, to have misgivings about the menu. She was not mistaken. The secretary, with a dramatic gesture, withdrew the lid from a pot that occupied the place of honor on the table, revealing a tepid, gray liquid in which swam a few morsels of potato.

In spite of her disappointment, and the discomforts of the lodgings, Alexandra did not leave the society, as she had firmly intended to do the day after her arrival. She provided her mattress, which rested directly on the floor, with the necessary bedding, and learned to avail herself of the public bath. The tiny woman, whom she described as "the most delicious idiot one could possibly imagine," aroused her sympathy.[5] She and her three-year-old child obviously suffered from mistreatment and lack of adequate nourishment. But Alexandra, who had a hearty appetite, immediately found a nearby restaurant to augment the Spartan regime.

Paris offered many opportunities for study. Courses in Sanskrit were available at the Sorbonne and the Collège de France, and she could benefit from contact with such eminent professors as Sylvain Lévi and Edouard Foucaux. It was the latter's translation of the Tibetan version of the *Lalita Vistara* that first introduced her to the Buddhism of Tibet. During this same year of 1888 she became a Freemason like her father, joining that long tradition of freethinkers including Wolfgang Amadeus Mozart, Goethe, and Benjamin Franklin.

The most important influence of the Paris years, however, came from the magnificent oriental collection housed in the Musée Guimet, considered exceptional to this day. The Musée Guimet contained within its walls more of mystery and esotericism than all those sects that offered childish and imaginary initiations to attract and delude so many unsuspecting fools.[6]

Alexandra attended a number of the evening "séances" over which M. Jourdan presided. She was unimpressed by the "vibrations" he elicited. She found the superficiality of the practices in which the group indulged and the lack of any real scholarship disappointing. With her customary intellectual independence, Alexandra was already going directly to the source for her inspiration. She devoted hours to examining the superb artifacts, paintings, sculptures, and tapestries gathered from all the countries of the Far East, and pored over the translations of sacred texts in the library. She was particularly moved by a magnificent Japanese Buddha that was installed in a niche overlooking the library. One evening she had remained late studying the texts and, believing herself to be alone, she saluted the figure in the oriental fashion, her palms joined together. A friendly but somewhat amused voice emanating from the shadows said, "May the blessing of Buddha be with you, Mademoiselle."[7] It was the Comtesse de Bréant who spoke. An intelligent and serious student of oriental philosophy, she spent many hours in the library.

Alexandra responded, "This very beautiful Japanese statue made me think of the great sage it is intended to resemble, and I salute the doctrine it represents."[8]

The comtesse immediately invited Alexandra to have tea with her. An opportunity to satisfy her *gourmandise* in a Parisian patisserie was too much of a temptation to refuse. As the limousine that awaited the comtesse at the museum's entrance swept them away, they were already engrossed in animated conversation. The two women discovered many interests in common. This aristocrat, who possessed a lively and vigorous intellect, had realized the dream so close to Alexandra's heart—a voyage to India. She introduced Alexandra to the Pythagorean Society, and they attended a number of lectures together at this cultural foundation. There Alexandra made the acquaintance of "le tout Paris" as far as occultism went, including an elderly Scottish eccentric, Lady Caithness, the Duchess of Pomar, who dabbled in "spiritism." The exotic decor of the hall in which the meetings were held proved to be an eclectic mixture of Greek and Egyptian temple architecture. The ceremonies played, for the most part, on a sense of the incredulous, and aroused superstitious beliefs stemming from varied traditions of antiquity. Psalms (of obscure origin) were chanted by the assembly, who then sat spellbound as an orator expounded on such subjects as "Number is the Essence of All Things." It was very much the mode during this period for the aristocracy of England and France to amuse themselves by means of contacting the "spirit world" for advice and consent, with astrology, alchemy, and a multitude of related subjects. In the provinces there were colonies in abundance where one might spend weeks or even years wandering through beautifully appointed gardens clad in filmy draperies, chanting a variety of texts selected at random from Egyptian, Greek, and Hindu sources. Dilettantism was the accepted approach. Dabbling in any number of exotic subjects was considered perfectly correct. One read "about," one "considered," and above all, one "discussed" (ad nauseum), with as much authority as one could muster, in the cafés or salons, depending on one's social position. The soirees of professors such as Sylvain Lévi were notable, and access to them jealously guarded. Japanese prints, Chinese porcelains, jade landscapes, and Persian miniatures filled the homes of wealthy collectors. These opulent interiors included masterpieces— screens, fans, low divans, mahogany tables, and niches containing Hindu deities. The great collections of Paris, London, Boston, and San Francisco were accumulated during this epoch. Evenings were often devoted to distractions such as *Thaïs*, *Aïda*, and *Madame Butterfly*, which combined, in addition to their oriental decor, irresistible elements of pathos, drama, opulence, and the woman-as-victim scenario. But to seriously consider any contact of a profound nature, to explore the deeper meaning of the philosophies that were associated with the artifacts, was a different matter altogether. To be sure, this point of view had a certain validity. For many innocent Westerners, to go further was to court disaster. In her letters Alexandra frequently referred to those ignorant and unsuspecting adepts who had disappeared in the quicksand of exotic experiences for which they were unprepared.

It is to Alexandra's credit that, engaged in examination and consideration, she was not tempted by the extravagant or the grotesque. She was able to discern how truly frivolous these groups were. Immersing herself in her Sanskrit studies, she prepared to embark for the land of her dreams to experience at first hand those attractions of which she could only read in London or Paris.

At the age of twenty-one, Alexandra had the right to claim a legacy from her godmother. Her parents naturally encouraged her to add it to their invested capital, to return home and live with them in relative comfort on the interest this would provide. Certainly such a conservative course would have been expected of a "normal" unmarried young woman, but it was the last thing Alexandra had in mind. Encouraged by her friend, Mme. de Bréant, she made immediate plans to embark for India. Her linguistic skills were adequate, and she had advanced as far as she could on the benches of a European university. She booked her passage at once.

For Alexandra this voyage was far from a tourist jaunt. It was a pilgrimage of the spirit. She had booked a single cabin, from which she intended to depart rarely, preferring hours of meditation and study to contact with the other passengers. The first evening she refused to answer the dinner gong. "I didn't wish to begin my mystical pilgrimage with the vulgar act of sitting down to eat."[9]

That night she sat on deck regarding the procession of

the planets in the sky above the slowly moving vessel. Suddenly a sensation of coolness penetrated her deep meditation, causing her to shiver. On the horizon, a rosy glimmer ascended gently into the dark sky, the day approached and, imperceptibly, she was aware that the great ship gliding toward the dawn was carrying her towards the Orient.[10]

She aroused a great curiosity among the other passengers. "Are you going to rejoin your family?" "No." When the word finally circulated that her purpose in going to India was to improve her knowledge of Sanskrit, she was left quite alone. She could pursue her studies in peace. These included the *Upanishads*, the *Bhagavad Gita*, and various Buddhist scriptures.

Arrivals were, in this period, free of formalities. Neither passports nor inoculations against tropical diseases were required. One simply debarked with one's belongings in hand. She touched ground in Ceylon at last, after a voyage of some fifteen days. Initially she felt much enthusiasm for this land where, according to legend, Adam had installed himself after the Expulsion, with the object of recreating his Paradise Lost. She secured lodgings in the nearest hotel, and dressed herself in the "uniform" chosen under the careful supervision of Mme. de Bréant. The costume *de rigueur* for a European woman in the Orient consisted of an impeccable white dress with long sleeves, white gloves, broad-brimmed hat, and the indispensable parasol. After fortifying herself with a cup of genuine Ceylon tea in a pavilion presided over by a portrait of Queen Victoria, she engaged a rickshaw, nicknamed *pousse-pousse* (push-push) by the French colonials,[11] and set off for the nearest Buddhist temple. After arriving, she lingered in the garden for some time, postponing the moment when she would confront her very first Buddhist shrine. At last she entered.

What she saw inside astonished her. On a narrow platform, surmounted by a baldequin, rested a larger than life-size statue that represented the Buddha at the moment of his death. This giant image was painted canary yellow. The clothing, the body, the face, and the hair were covered with the same vivid enamel. Near the head of the dying Sage one of the faithful had placed a package of toothpicks and a pocket handkerchief was suspended from the baldequin. A glass jar containing an offering of artistically preserved carrots and peas completed the display.[12]

The shock to her aesthetic sensibilities, nourished among the masterpieces of the Musée Guimet, of seeing a religious image lacquered like a piece of garden furniture, was so great she began to feel dizzy. Returning to her rickshaw, she commanded the driver to return at once to the hotel.

The next morning, after a good night's sleep, she decided to try again. This time she asked the opinion of the hotel manager regarding Buddhist shrines. He advised her to visit the temple complex of Kelinaya, located several kilometers from Colombo. It proved to be fully satisfying, an assembly of buildings dominated at the center by a large temple. The silence that prevailed in this remote place created an ambience of serenity and withdrawal from the cares of the world. This was more what she had expected. The interior of the temple was appropriately somber and, as her eyes became accustomed to the darkness, she could distinguish an effigy resting behind a glass partition. It was a similar representation, a favorite in Ceylon it seemed, of the parinirvana of the Buddha. And unbelievably, this one had also been completely varnished with the same canary yellow enamel, the full length of its more than five meters. Once again she experienced an enormous disappointment.

Much later she had the opportunity to discuss with native artists the representations of the Buddha presented in so many temples. It seemed the artists confused impassiveness and serenity with a complete absence of expression. This often resulted in forms without any life.

It is true also that Western museums favored examples of the Gandhara school, in which for the first time the Buddha was represented as a human figure, rather than by a footprint or a parasol. These were the work of sculptors influenced by the Greek artisans who had penetrated western India after the conquest of Alexander the Great, and met the representational standards of the West. Once this visual precedent had become established, it rendered subsequent (and more authentic) images "primitive" to the eyes of Europeans.

At one end of the glass case containing the figure of the Buddha, she noticed a multitude of miniature bowls, such as one would find in a doll's house. The sacristan explained to Alexandra that a faithful Buddhist who had vowed to make an offering of fifty or a hundred bowls of milk in recompense for a prayer that had been answered to his satisfaction would economize by using these tiny containers. She saluted the sleeping Buddha with a ritual prostration, thinking of the other in Paris.[13]

Alexandra assuaged this initial disillusionment with the thought that this was only the beginning. India awaited across the Bay of Tuticorin.

The distance was not very long, but the crossing proved to be one of the most traumatic experiences of her life. The boat was the "size of a nutshell," and the first-class section consisted of a tiny dining room, off of which were six small cabins. As soon as they left the security of the port, the sea became very turbulent. The portholes were closed, and the cabins became suffocating. Dinner was out of the question. The fragile ship was being tossed about so alarmingly that Alexandra and the three Catholic priests who were her companions in first class made for the security of their cabins. Soon waves were crashing over the sides of the lower decks, and the craft was shuddering as though in extremis. All at once the upper decks were invaded by enormous rats that poured out of their holes below decks and into the cabins, accompanied by myriad insects. Giant cockroaches, lice, and spiders soon covered the walls, the curtains, and the carpet, and filled the wash basin to overflowing. Alexandra, thrown from one side of the cabin to the other, overwhelmed by nausea, hadn't the force to push them away, and was soon herself covered from head to foot with vermin. Suddenly her attention was gripped by unearthly screams that seemed to mount from the bowels of hell itself. The deck passengers had been forced into an enclosure to prevent their being swept overboard by the crashing waves. They were convinced the boat was about to sink, carrying them with it. This Dantesque nightmare continued during the entire crossing, until they dropped anchor in Tuticorin. The rats and vermin recovered their nests, and the unfortunate ship vomited its miserable cargo onto the beach. For Alexandra, it was an experience of horror she would remember all her life.

Once on shore, however, she regained her composure along with her stability, donned her immaculate tropical "whites," installed herself in the first-class compartment of the waiting train, and demanded breakfast—a vegetable curry with generous helpings of toast and strong tea. This she devoured on the way to Madoura, to the utter dismay of one of the priests who had the misfortune to share her quarters.

The railway stations in India at this time were equipped with separate waiting rooms for women. There it was possible not only to bathe in cool water, but to receive a massage from one of the women attendants. On her arrival in Madoura, Alexandra availed herself of this comfort, then fell asleep in the adjacent women's dormitory. No event, however catastrophic, seemed to diminish her hearty appetite or her ability to sleep.

Her route followed the more or less classic tourist itinerary of the time, including Madras and Benares. Few details are available to us. However, one encounter of great importance took place in a rose garden in Benares. There she was received by Swami Bashkarananda, an aged ascetic who spent the entire year, including the cold winter months, seated in meditation without clothes, and protected only by a makeshift shelter. His devoted followers tended the rose garden surrounding him, and ministered to his simple needs. It was a relationship that Alexandra would see over and over again in India. Swami Bashkarananda was perhaps not truly erudite, although he had written several treatises on Vedantist philosophy, but he possessed a penetrating understanding of Indian thought, to which he initiated her in her twenty-fifth year.[14]

They discussed the cloistered life of those committed to a religious vocation in the West, which he found astonishing. What need was there for those high walls? One cannot help remembering the drawing of the six-year-old Alexandra. The thin tissue of an orange robe seemed to the Indian sage to be a sufficient protection for one who walked a path away from the world. When Alexandra departed, he placed a ritual scarf about her shoulders, and whispered a few words in her ear.

Many years later she revisited the garden, in which roses no longer bloomed. A mausoleum had been erected over Bashkarananda's habitual place of meditation. His followers had reverently interred him in the lotus position, as was customary for a holy man. The small edifice was already beginning to show signs of decay. Since he had made no effort to organize his community, it too had dissolved, and few there were to decorate his tomb with garlands. A layer of dust covered everything, and weeds had taken over the paths of the once immaculate garden. As she respectfully bowed before the sage's tomb, a flood of memories poured through her mind, and she heard again the whispered words, "Impermanence is the universal law."[15]

3

Beside the Other Life

«1893~1900»

Alexandra returned from India without a penny. She had spent her entire inheritance. Her father, now seventy-eight, had never shown great ability as an investor, and his holdings had fallen greatly in value. The principal sources of revenue for the family were now the fabric boutiques inherited by Mme. David. She was still hopeful that Alexandra would take her place as a manager of one of these concessions. For a brief period Alexandra had tried her hand at shopkeeping, but quickly gave up, realizing that she simply did not have the mentality it required. The alternatives for an unmarried woman of twenty-five were few. Although she had published a number of articles about her Indian experience in scholarly journals, she was paid little for them, and philosophy as a career did not provide a living.

For many young women of good family who were forced to support themselves, there was music. Vocal and piano studies were usually included in the education of upperclass women. Alexandra had shown not only enthusiasm but considerable talent at the piano, and possessed a pleasing soprano voice that merited further training. At the age of twenty-five she enrolled in the Conservatory of Brussels. Soon she moved back to Paris, where she felt the conservatory had more to offer, and where she could make more progress. She completed her studies, winning all the prizes and, what must have been the

greatest reward of all, her mother's response: "I salute
you, Great Artist!"

A great artist Alexandra probably was not. She had
made a late start, and the life of a soprano is relatively
short. The other obstacle to a successful theatrical career was her determination to succeed on the strength of
her vocal and dramatic talent, instead of riding on the
favors of important men—a feminist point of view considered not only "original" but disastrous at the time.
She spent long hours in musty anterooms waiting to
demonstrate her talent before indifferent directors. After weeks of exhausting auditions, she found a well-
paying position as the *première cantatrice* in the Opera
Company of Hanoi. Her parents were very proud of her
status as a true professional, and she was allowed to
return to the Orient she so loved. Subsequently she sang
in Athens, North Africa, and the French provinces, but
her coveted goal, the Opéra de Paris, she never attained.

The period between 1893 and 1900, during which she
followed her musical career, is described by Alexandra
in an autobiographical novel entitled *Le Grand Art—
journal d'une actrice*, which she finished in 1902 and
offered for publication. On the eve of her marriage to
Philippe Néel she must have decided it was too candid a
revelation of her private life, and she withdrew it from
publication. After her death, Marie-Ma discovered it
hidden in the back of a closet, a volume of eight hundred
handwritten pages tied with a ribbon, and covered with
much dust. It was signed "Alexandra Myrial," a *nom de
plume* suggested by "M. Myrial" in *Les Miserables* by
Victor Hugo. Alexandra published under this name for
a number of years.

Concealed within a tedious and often banal account of
the manners and morals of the theater at that time is a
revelation of Alexandra's interior life—her fears, her
aspirations, above all her struggle to suppress her awakening sensuality.

As her heroine, Cecile, Alexandra describes the epi-

sode that first aroused her ambition to become a singer.
She attends a performance of Gounod's opera *Faust* in
the company of her mother. The music has inspired her,
and awakened all her latent ambition and desire. Walking beside her mother in the darkness after they have
left the concert hall, she muses:

"Art will give me a life 'beside' the other life . . . make
me forget the ugliness of life . . . allow me to satisfy my
thirst for the beautiful, the heroic, the grandiose, that
nothing seems to satisfy."[1]

Although it possesses little artistic merit, *Le Grand
Art* is of interest as another self-portrait of Alexandra.
It represents an exorcism of the hopes, fears, ambitions,
and disappointments she experienced during her years
as an operatic soprano. She examined the episodes in all
their grotesque detail, then, laying them on a shelf in the
back of her life, she went on to other pursuits.

In the story, the heroine, Cecile, is left without resources when the theatrical company, of which she is the
star, closes its doors. To survive, she surrenders herself
to the embraces of a loathsome provincial cattle dealer,
who takes her home to the rustic discomforts of his farm.
During the interminable winter months of freezing rain
and fog she is virtually a prisoner in this place, enduring
with pain and disgust the clumsy, drunken abuse of the
crude peasant. To ease the misery of her isolation, she
recounts her life in retrospect, her years of performing
in the provinces, in Hanoi, Athens, Paris. The saga
unfolds in the context of endlessly repeated romantic
disappointments.

"There will always be men, gaily libertine or cynically
brutal, staring at me, undressing me with their eyes,
sizing up my flesh, reckoning how much pleasure I might
give them."[2]

"Misery of woman, poor or too weak, who lives only
for a man, who gives herself because of pity, or charity,
or compassion, or gratitude—so frequently wounded

because her heart is without defense against the 'master' who seems loving and gentle.''[3]

Whether the images Alexandra evokes of unwashed, sweaty bodies, foul breath, and murmured obscenities emerge from the shadows of what had been witnessed, overheard, or imagined, she responded with nausea and revulsion. If they represent her fantasies, they indicate a pathological rejection of her own awakening sensuality. Everything physical is represented as filthy, disgusting, and above all, masculine.

In his well-researched biography *Le Lumineux destin d'Alexandra David-Néel*, Jean Chalon comments that during this period in her life Alexandra lived quite openly with Jean Haustont, a Belgian composer she met through the Paris Theosophical Society.[4] According to Chalon, they occupied an apartment in Passy, as "M. et Mme. Myrial," and traveled extensively together. Jean is referred to frequently in the letters she received from Elisée Reclus, a mentor and friend in Brussels. Since her father also refers to him in his letters to Alexandra, it would seem that their relationship was known and apparently accepted by M. David. Jean was a composer of promise (they created together a short operetta), and had an interest in the music of the Orient. He prepared a detailed pamphlet on Buddhist processionals and, influenced by Chinese music, invented a new system of tonality. As an innovative composer he was well ahead of his time. In her notes, Alexandra usually refers to him as "H," and this letter continues to punctuate her engagement diary for many years. Presumably Alexandra left Jean when she was offered an opportunity to sing in Athens, but they remained friends. As "Cecile" she falls deeply in love with "Pierre," a frail, withdrawn pianist, whose physical description could well represent Haustont. Alexandra describes the maternal and protective feelings she must have had for Jean. "But Pierre was my child, for whom I wanted to make existence beautiful, happy, my child for whom I would have given my life, and this feeling would not die."[5]

Possibly it was the nostalgic memory of the life led by "M. et Mme. Myrial" at 3, rue Nicolo in Passy that provided the background for the few idyllic episodes in *Le Grand Art*.

Her reaction to sexual encounters is one of disgust. As Cecile she is the silent witness to the erotic maneuvers of a fellow artist who occupies an adjoining room. They are described with candor and explicit detail. She justifies the voyeurism on the grounds she would like to learn a few tricks herself, but her reaction is one of loathing. In all these more than eight hundred pages filled with resentment, unfulfilled longing, and the desire for revenge, there is only one passage that speaks of gentleness and compassion. When Cecile at last confronts her tormenter, the rage that has been choking her evaporates. She sees tears glistening on his rough, unshaven face. The words she had longed to scream at him are forgotten. Sadly she shakes her head, and gives him, instead of the blow she had so long prepared, a gentle kiss on his rough cheek.

The climax of the novel is an opening-night production at the Opéra de Paris in which the heroine plays the title role in *Thaïs*. *Thaïs* is the creation of two of Alexandra's favorites, the novelist Anatole France and the composer Jules Massenet. It is clear that, of all the roles she had performed during her operatic career, she most identified with Thaïs. The story takes place in fourth-century Alexandria, Egypt, where Thaïs, a famous courtesan, has become the favorite of the intellectuals and philosophers. She is abducted by a Christian fanatic, who secretly lusts for her, and who incarcerates her in a desert monastery to expiate her sins. There, to distract herself, she creates music with a small flute. This music is of such transcendent beauty that the seal on her door breaks, and she is free. After a life devoted to religious teaching, she dies a saint. The fanatic, whose one desire has been to seduce her, commits suicide. It is a story that plays heavily on themes dear to the heart of Alexandra—the integration of the sensual and the spiritual, the love of ceremony and exotic display, the desire to be a favorite among the intellectuals of her time, and the power of art, specifically music, to evoke feeling.

The shadow of *Thaïs* lingered with Alexandra for many years. On July 26, 1969, as Marie-Ma carried Alexandra's breakfast into her room, she was greeted by a forceful, operatic voice: "Father, God has spoken to me. He has created in my soul a great light, and I saw the emptiness of all that I have been." Marie-Ma, not unused to dramatic greetings, inquired, "You wrote that, Madame?" "No," came the reply, "it is *Thaïs* by Anatole France, and believe me, 'Tortue,' that man knew how to write!"[6]

Like a series of Chinese dolls, Alexandra creates a sequence of scenarios within scenarios in this wearisome but still intriguing autobiographical work. If her evocations on stage were as moving as these literary descriptions, it is unfortunate that her dramatic career did not last longer. But the "life beside the other life" had been consumed. In other settings, however, her career as an actress continued. Having discovered that "all the world's a stage," she began to enlarge her repertoire.

4

Philippe

«1900-1911»

In 1904 Philippe Néel received a response to a letter he had recently written to an elderly gentleman whom he would never meet, Louis David. "Your letter caused me great astonishment. Until today, my daughter had shown such a firm determination never to forgo her liberty, and had constantly protested against the inferior state that the law imposes on a woman in all the acts of her life after marriage. Your letter today has led me to believe that Alexandra has strongly modified her ideas, and if this is so, Monsieur, I see no reason to refuse my consent to an honorable union. . . ."[1]

Monsieur Philippe Néel had been duly warned. Her father knew from years of experience that there was little chance his daughter had really changed her mind. The reasoning behind her decision to marry Philippe Néel remained a mystery to everyone, perhaps even to Alexandra herself. But it is worth examining the alternatives open to a thirty-six-year-old woman of that period. She had harvested a certain acclaim, as well as financial stability, from her operatic career, but she was wise enough to recognize that the end was in sight. She would grace the center stage of the Opéra de Paris only in *Le Grand Art*. As a writer and lecturer she had begun to attract an interested following, both in Brussels and Paris. Her diary for 1900 refers to many literary projects.[2] But in this period, even in the most erudite literary circles the writing of an unmarried woman was not taken very seriously. The presence of a husband was required for entry into the "serious" world of arts and letters. From an economic point of view writing provided no more than a subsistence, if that. For women at this time, even those with independent means, the options remained those open to them for centuries: marriage, the church, or caring for elderly parents.

Alexandra had moved to the other side of the footlights, having been offered the directorship of the casino of Tunis. As she became aware that her voice was diminishing, she was delighted to accept a position that would provide continued financial independence and allow her to remain in the theatrical world she knew and understood. It was in the casino that she made the acquaintance of a frequent patron, Philippe Néel. A friendship developed rapidly, and she recorded her first voyage on board his yacht September 15, 1900: " 'Hirondelle'— first sailing."[3]

In her novel Philippe is thinly disguised as two quite different men. First, he is Georges, the son of a baron, handsome, seductive, well spoken, and completely assured, who amuses himself by pretending to love Cecile. He is also present in the guise of Bernheim, the protector, a man of the world, a father-figure, a man who loves to spoil little girls. He might have, in fact did step out of a fading actress's dream. So, from the very beginning, Philippe was cast as both the seducer and the solution. For a long time, Alexandra vacillated about marriage, preferring to play the role of mistress. Her feelings about matrimony were clearly set forth in the notes she entered in her diary in February 1900. "Title of book: *Woman in Love and Marriage*—this terrain is a battlefield between the sexes. The expressions of familiar language: 'to make a conquest,' 'to be a happy conqueror,' to let oneself 'be overcome,' etc., as if it were a battle in which the male aggressor forces the female to give in against her desire."[4]

But her relationship with Jean Haustont, which did

not seem to fit this stereotype, did not last. The actual
end of their relationship remained obscure. Alexandra
never spoke of it, but it was rumored that, while she
fulfilled a lengthy singing engagement in Athens, another
had taken her place. Philippe, on the other hand,
couldn't have better fitted her script. At forty, he was
considered the catch of the year, handsome, desirable,
well-to-do, and, like "Georges," he had the reputation
of being a notorious philanderer. Born in Alès in the
Gard (not far from the famous Pont), his lineage was
aristocratic. A brilliant student, he graduated as an
engineer, and became chief engineer of the Chemin de
Fer d'Afrique du Nord. He was used to possessing authority, used to having his way, used to finding quick
solutions to practical problems. He lived his life with
passion and enthusiasm. He did not waste valuable time
examining his motives for desiring to marry Alexandra.
As a woman of the world she certainly understood the
context of marriage as it existed at this time. As Alain
Decaux remarks, "The husband of 1900, similar to that
of the Second Empire, satisfied his sexual needs in other
places than the marital bed."[5]

Alexandra was much photographed during these years
and though not what one would describe as a beauty,
she was elegant and assured. Her diary is filled with
appointments with couturiers, and she made frequent
shopping expeditions to Paris. Her wardrobe, chosen
with care, displayed now the last word in Paris chic, now
an oriental exoticism. For Philippe, beginning at last to
have his fill of the mindless coquettes who threw themselves at him, she presented something of a challenge.
She was an original model, not one of a series, which
appealed to his instincts as a "collector." As she appeared to be less and less convinced that marriage was
what she wanted, he pressed his suit with more determination. In her diary for February 3, 1904, she indulged
in a long tirade against Philippe and his numerous
affairs. She had apparently come across some souvenirs,

notes, handkerchiefs, et cetera, which put her in a
veritable fury of jealousy. She had discovered that Philippe's invitations to board the "Hirondelle" merited
always the same follow-up of a postcard of the yacht,
and a little poem that was not distinguished by its
originality. Although this behavior was quite typical of a
well-to-do man of the world, to her it seemed petty,
frivolous, and demeaning, and she was enraged to think
she had herself been so easily deceived. Of course, she
should have known better, but it would seem that the
realistic Alexandra possessed a romantic side to her
character. It is clear that she knew, well in advance,
what kind of man she was marrying—a man whose
appetites and tastes (and the means of satisfying them)
in no way differed from the majority of men of his social
class. When she noted on August 4, 1904, "I married
that horrible Alouch[6] at the French consultate in Tunis,"
she was following her own script. She seemed to believe
that Philippe had pursuaded her to abandon her usual
independent stance.

After the wedding they left for a brief tour of France.
Then the bridegroom returned to Tunis and Alexandra
was called to Paris by the demands of her literary career.
As she was about to rejoin him, she received word that
would gravely affect the course of her marriage. Her
father was seriously ill. She hastened at once to Brussels.

As she had matured, Alexandra had appreciated her
father more and more. During the years she had traveled
as a singer, they had seen little of each other, but he had
written her long, affectionate letters, filled with fatherly
affection and advice. She was still his adored "Nini,"
whom he longed to see more often, but whose caprices
he accepted in good grace. Alexandra could never claim
that her father was not supportive of what must have
seemed, to an elderly gentleman, puzzling behavior. He
accepted (and applauded) her musical career, he accepted her relationship with Jean Haustont, he accepted
her spontaneous arrivals and departures and constantly

changing itineraries. He accepted Philippe, whom he never met. Few paternal figures of this period would have responded with sympathy to a daughter who persisted in such untraditional behavior, but she knew his true feelings. Of course, he lectured her on questions of health and hygiene, but that was an indication of how much he cared. He missed the long discussions they had had on the many subjects of mutual interest, philosophy, history, and politics. Undoubtedly his approval for this very respectable match had influenced her decision to marry. On the eve of her marriage he had written: "Adieu, dearest Nini. Your mother and your father send their wishes for happiness and their congratulations on the threshold of the new and brilliant life that opens to you."[7]

The weeks she spent in Brussels as he was dying must have aroused emotions that were almost insupportable. She wrote Philippe a revealing letter that said she would not waste herself on small sentimentalities, but she was capable of a great love for one who seemed worthy, who could love her in the same way.[8] Her father alone qualified as being "worthy" of her great love. There could be no competing with him. Till this point in her life her relationships with men had been determined by this fact.

The last few weeks of his life were indeed painful. Her mother was hysterical and helpless by turns. There were endless financial crises, which were solved by requesting bank drafts from Philippe. There were days when she wanted desperately to escape and return to Tunis. She wrote with genuine affection and longing for her "Alouch." She was distraught, depressed, angry, and carrying the burden of a grief she would not have imagined possible. Finally it was over. Adieu, dearest Nini.

"My father was buried at Ucele. He was placed in his coffin at ten A.M. I left the house at seven P.M. and installed myself *chez* Elisée Reclus."[9] For the first time Alexandra was forced to confront the loss of one whose

love she truly appreciated only at the moment of separation. The years following her marriage and the death
of her father represented for Alexandra the dark night
of the soul. Her days were filled with a frenzy of activity—lectures, articles, correspondence, luncheons, dinners, concerts, and frequent excursions into the nearby
desert. In 1905 Alexandra and Philippe were photographed on the terrace of their North African villa,
handsome, well turned-out (she is wearing her favorite
Japanese kimono), the ideal bourgeois couple. But rarely
was she in such repose, never was she content.

She continued to send articles to the journals. In 1905
she wrote on "Moukden—notes historiques" for *Mercure*
of Paris, and gave a lecture on "La Morale Laique"
before the Congress of Free Thought, in which she
stressed that freethinkers should never impose a system
of morality (in competition with the Church, for in-
stance), but should support only that moral code which
emerges from reasoned, scientific demonstration. She
stressed the importance of improved public education to
further this end. But her thoughts strayed often in the
direction of her deteriorating relationship with Philippe.
In the same year of 1905, she noted in her diary on
August nineteenth: "Paris: evening, under a window in
the shadow of the church, a man and woman caress each
other. My thoughts were aroused and a sudden disgust
toward N. Why is it that my life's companion should be
associated only with obscene ideas, that I imagine him
only with repugnant gestures? What misery!"[10]

In January 1906 there is a note: "Responded to H.
(Haustont) for copies of 'Lidia.'[11] This was the operetta
on which they had collaborated. May thirty-first found
her in Rome attending the first Congress of Women,
which she found disappointing. The activists of that day
were not up to her high standards. On New Year's Day,
1907, she invoked: "Invisible companion present always
during my lonely youth . . . descend toward me in my
distress."[12] Was she longing for her father?

It is not surprising that her health began to decline under all this pressure. There are increasing notations concerning her recurring "neurasthenia" (as nervousness was then called), headaches, nausea, and other discomforts. She went to the spas and mountains for cures that were never successful. She succumbed to periods of nostalgia. On January fifteenth she wrote that she had recognized a former tenor she knew in Athens. She would so like to have talked with him about the old days . . . but to what profit? She had become a bourgeoise of Tunis. "All that is buried. . . . Oh, joyous hours, painful hours, hours of living. Ah, youth!"[13]

On April twenty-eighth she commented that her marriage had brought on premature age. She saw, in her mirror, a resemblance to her mother, which appalled her. She believed her life was over.

But her diary is full of recorded activity. On August 19, 1907, she reports that her article "Marriage—Profession for Women" has appeared in *La Société nouvelle*. September twenty-third she is in Geneva—"très neurasthenique." October tenth, in Paris, she attends *Madame Butterfly* at the Opéra Comique. In 1908, under the name of Alexandra David (she no longer used the name "Myrial"), she wrote for *La Fronde*, "The Liberation of Women from the Weight of Maternity." The happiest events she noted were musical. February 11, 1909, it is the Trio Baroiz from Spain—"truly marvelous!" The luncheons, dinners, tea parties, meetings, lectures continued in an unabated stream—also the headaches, the loss of appetite, the fatigue. She wrote on every conceivable subject—the Zionists in Palestine, Buddhism, rational feminism. When in Paris she frequented the salons, where many erudite scholars gathered around her as she spoke of what she considered to be a "living" Hindu philosophy. Her theories were well in advance of her time, when all intellectual investigation implied maintaining a discreet distance from the material under observation. One was expected to concern

oneself only with the so-called "facts" about the subject:
the age of the documents, the place of birth, the possible
historical existence of the philosophers and teachers,
and the influence and impact of historical events. To take
the ideas themselves seriously, or to go so far as to
participate in a religious experience oneself, was considered unsuitable in the context of Western investigation.
To observe was permitted, but not to participate.

In 1910 she spent some time in England to support
rallies for women's suffrage, and lectured before the
London Buddhist Society. She then went on to Edin-
burgh to speak. This was followed in November by a
series of lectures at the Université Nouvelle in Brussels.
Buddhism was assuming a more and more important
place in her life—both professional and private. Her
book *Le Modernisme bouddhiste et le bouddhisme du
Bouddha* was ready for publication. Possibly the fact
that she was able to survive these dark years and emerge
emotionally intact can be attributed to her increasing
involvement with the Middle Way of Siddhartha Gau-
tama. She mentioned in her diary "the delicious hour of
perfect detachment and intimate joy" when she knelt
before her own shrine and meditated before the golden
image of the Buddha gleaming softly in the light of an
altar lamp.[14] For a brief period at least, her tired mind
could find surcease from the endless round of questioning she imposed upon it. Alexandra had set herself on a
course from which there seemed to be no possibility of
turning. Feelings had been aroused that threatened to
destroy her if they were not rigorously repressed. She
filled her days and nights with an obsessed frenzy of
activity that consumed all her energy. She had lost
Haustont, her "child"; she had lost Louis David, her
first and greatest love. Philippe could in no way replace
either one of them. Shortly after their marriage she had
commented to him that they had made a peculiar marriage and had married more out of spite than tenderness.

She revealed to him that he was not the kind of companion she had dreamed of and that she was even less the kind of wife he needed.[15]

She who had always prided herself on her ability to face reality lamented, "Fantasy alone is desirable."[16] But it would seem she could no longer indulge even in that escape. Her muse was silent, her body was rebelling, her mind in torment. For the first time in her life she was not in complete control.

Philippe responded with complete honesty. In an undated letter written to Alexandra when she was at Lourdes, he wrote: "I don't know if you really understand me. I have a soul that is very bourgeois, and very stupid. A bourgeois life would have suited me. You are the antithesis of that. Others have told you that, and they are right. Therefore, what shall we do with this relationship that we have created? . . . I am attached to you by legal ties easy to break, and by others out of habit. If your life with me is too difficult . . . I am willing to give you your liberty. . . . Tell me if you believe we should truly continue side by side, or if we should each go where the wind blows us. Adieu, my dear wife."[17]

The idea that she would rebel against the very comfortable life he had provided must have come as a shock to him. In the context of French society she had everything—money, social position, above all, the attention that only a married woman could command. And there is a side of her, revealed in the letters of this period, that very much wanted the relationship to work. At times she had feelings of deep affection for her husband. It was the ambivalence in her attitude that tore her apart, and caused her health to decline.

"October 7, 1904, Paris—I love you very much, my dearest, with all my heart. My life is, I promise you, from now on entirely oriented with yours, thinking only of walking happily side by side a very long time."[18]

"December 23, 1904, Brussels—I have been so touched by the solicitude you have shown toward me since I have been here and I hope so much to come, a very little girl, and rest against your shoulder."

"September 22, 1906, Ealing, England—My dear Al-ouch . . . I will return to you with great joy, if you wish. . . . I am completely different from the way you know me to be . . . from the way you have forced me to be. If you only knew, my friend, what great desire I have that we could be good companions for each other. . . . Perhaps if we no longer played the 'roles,' if we could be simply ourselves as we were before we met, we could reach an understanding, a new accord, happy this time, and lasting. . . . I know that I would like to be close to you. Welcome me, dear Mouchy. I will come to you with all my heart. It is not our names written on a register that makes us husband and wife. I would hope that we could, after a long experience of loyalty, say to each other, 'I would like to spend my life with you,' and this day will be truly our wedding day."

More than once during her constant voyaging she remarked how he surpassed in every way the husbands of her friends, and the other men she encountered. She would enumerate his good qualities with sincere appreciation. The problem was not Philippe. The problem was marriage. She was incapable of making space in her life for another person. Furthermore, she could not afford the risk. The maternal rejection she had experienced in the beginning of her life—in the first days, even—had forged her character. She had learned that survival demands being able to stand alone. She could fantasize, and even express her longing for affection, for companionship. She could say how much she wanted to rest her head on Mouchy's solid shoulder and be comforted against the inner torments that plagued her. But this could happen only when they were separated by many miles. Certainly the unfortunate coincidence of her father's death following so soon after her marriage had an impact. She acknowledged herself that "the death of my father has truly struck a blow to my spirit."[19] Sensing, even as a very young child, that everything about her was a disappointment to her mother, her recourse was to turn to the only other human being available to her, her father. Over the years she had created with this withdrawn intellectual a substitute relationship. His death not only deprived her, it reminded her of the earlier, even more traumatic loss of her mother's affection. Never again, never again, must she allow that to happen.

Monday, August 1, 1910, after she had finished copying *Le Bouddhisme du Bouddha*, 508 pages. She wrote, "From all this wisdom I've amassed, have I gleaned anything? To the Path I have watched unfold, and in which I have in my spirit such complete faith, will the attraction be in vain? I can only say with the Dharma: not according to my desire, nor for my own success, nor to satisfy my vanity, but for the good, the happiness, and the salvation of the greatest number."[20]

She had carried her study as far as she possibly could on her own. The attraction of the Orient was stronger than it had ever been. She must have realized, however unconsciously, that her survival lay in that direction. Philippe, for his part, had offered her "a long voyage," hoping that she would, once and for all, "get it out of her system" and become the wife he very much wanted. The last page of her diary for 1910 bears a title: "On the Threshold of Nirvana—a good title for a book of travels across the Buddhist Orient."

So it was that when Mouchy arrived at Vichy in the late summer of that year for his annual "cure," he found a letter waiting for him. "Marseille, August 12, 1911. This word brings you my affectionate thoughts when I will be already far away on the sea, moving toward Egypt, on the threshold of the other Orient, and ready for the plunge. I wish you a happy vacation, a good stay in Vichy, rest and distraction. In my heart I am with you, my dear Mouchy, and I enclose in this note a loving kiss of welcome."[21]

She had left.

5

The Search Begins

«1911~1912»

On August 10, 1911, Alexandra wrote to her husband that the weather, as he had predicted, was beautiful, and so mild that she was able to write to him from the deck. The ship, however, was the filthiest she had ever seen.[1]

Alexandra's adventuring was frequently punctuated by colorful accounts of the filth she encountered. Rarely did she suffer in silence, nor did she soften the impact of the details with delicate language. The decks of the ship were littered with cigar butts and the rotting remains of third-class passengers' meals. The extreme heat was oppressive, she was feverish, and she believed she had fainted on regaining her cabin the previous evening. When she awoke at five o'clock in the morning, she was still clutching the objects she had picked up as she was about to retire.

In spite of having realized at long last the dream that had obsessed her for so many years, she acknowledged her second thoughts. It had even occurred to her to leave for Vichy and surprise Philippe there. But after much reflection she realized that pain always follows those actions that are not carefully screened by reason, and decided that it would not be reasonable now to renounce the trip planned for such a long time.[2]

Alexandra was in the precarious position of a trapeze artist in midair. She had left behind her security, her comfort, and a certain renown. Ahead of her the route

(43)

she had chosen was veiled by obscurity. And, resolute as she was, her very real affection for Philippe, which appeared to assert itself most strongly when they were separated, continued to distract her. To overcome her nostalgia, she recalled the ambition by which she had been driven for so many years. Alexandra's goal was to bring life to her research, to make her readers aware of how she had seen, touched, and felt those things that she recounted so vividly. She believed she had much more to offer than many of the intellectuals in vogue at the time. It was also obvious that she had little use for that modesty then considered so very essential to the comportment of a well-born woman. Had that been an important consideration, she would not have been writing from the deck of a steamer heading eastward across the Mediterranean. Even her expressions of insupportable egotism were frequently followed by a disarming candor. She finished this first letter with: "But all this—true, justifiable, and reasonable as it may be, does not prevent my retaining before my eyes the image of a Mouchy standing on the *quai* of Bizerte, a silhouette I watched for such a long time, as it disappeared in the night. My dearest Alouch, we are composed of many different cells, which pursue their lives in us, and how varied are the feelings that we experience. I have always been one who is rational. There are those who believe that to be madness."[3]

There existed between these two a complex bond. Though attenuated by time and distance, it survived. Over a period of thirty years, in the midst of all her exotic adventures, dangers, and discomforts, Alexandra found the time each day to take out her paper and pen. Whether she composed her letter on the deck of a ship, in the crowded compartment of a swaying train, or under the protective branches of one of "her" trees, Mouchy was there for her. He had the power to extract those thoughts she shared with no one else, and provided the canvas on which she projected her visions, her fears, her ambitions. Though far away, he was omnipresent. She allowed herself a great freedom of expression in these letters. There is an effortless progression of ideas and images, and the very rhythm of her movement is reflected in the flow of her evocative descriptions.

Ceylon was noted in her diary with a certain brevity. On September 7th she visited two Buddhist temples under the full moon, not mentioning whether the images of the Buddha were lacquered with brilliant citron as before. But on the ninth when she went to spend some time in a Theosophist center to concentrate on her Pali language studies, she was delighted with the ancient statue that graced the temple there. Brought from India, it dated from the time of Ashoka. She had hoped to make numerous excursions into the mountains, but traveling was rendered more difficult than usual by torrential rains, and she began to feel discouraged. Things did not seem equal to her expectations. She recounted with pleasure the opportunity to sit alone for two delicious hours, watching the faithful circling the Bo tree in the misty twilight. But moments of reflection were infrequent. Letters of introduction had preceded her from France, and she had already become a celebrity. An immense curiosity had arisen about this most unusual Parisian who had dared to become a serious seeker. There were many obligations, people to see, meetings and interviews pressed upon her. The solitude she so cherished was frequently interrupted.

Her arrival in India was a shock. In twenty years things had changed. And Alexandra had changed as well. Instead of bouncing precariously across the Bay of Tuticorin in a minuscule boat, swept along by a hurricane, she embarked at Colombo in a large, comfortable steamer, and saw, as they drew into the harbor at Tuticorin, a port much like that in any other part of the world. Her youthful recollections were dampened as well by the fact that her arrival coincided with the rainy season. She longed for the India that used to be, burning under a terrible green sky, and the dusty roads where clouds of powder had permeated the rosy twilight.[4]

Alexandra was not one to accept discouragement, however. She immersed herself at once in the Hindu world that had intrigued her for so long, and forgot her physical discomfort. With vivid, painterly strokes she recreates a procession she witnessed in Mandapan. Tall men, their foreheads painted symbolically red and white, their naked bodies streaked with ashes, trotted with quick, agile steps, as they bore the heavy palanquins on which rested the figures of the gods. Each one carried in his free hand a kind of torch, which created the illusion that he held the fire itself in his hand. She was overwhelmed by the eerie, diffused light that enveloped the stark figures, and the unearthly moaning of the trumpets that accompanied this ritual. Their tonalities evoked for her the domain of the "Other," as it was known during the Middle Ages in Europe, and she was transported by the vision even to the point of identifying with the patterned red and white flowers crushed beneath the fast-moving procession. For her it was an unforgettable vision and she would have liked to remain a long time absorbing the atmosphere.[5]

With a gifted reporter's eye for details, she notes an erect, naked black man, carrying on his head a case of "gazouze" (club soda), strolling nonchalantly along the platform where she was waiting for her train. She had ample opportunity for such observations. Pauses between trains were often interminable, forcing her at times to sleep in the crowded waiting rooms. The separate "ladies' quarters" she had enjoyed previously no longer existed, and she was forced to endure a proximity she found most uncomfortable. Schedules were precarious at best, and a traveling maharajah might delay a departure for some time. More than once her sleep was interrupted by the cheering crowds that invariably surrounded these colorful departures.

During the journey by train from Trichinopoli to

Adyar-Madras on November 22nd, a Brahman entered her compartment. She lost no time in drawing from her sack a copy of the *Bhagavad Gita*. This resulted not only in a lively discussion, but an invitation to continue the conversation as a guest in his home, an exceptional event, since the rules of their caste forbade the Brahmans from receiving strangers. The encounter, to which her friend invited the professor who expounded the Vedas in the local temple, took place in the inner patio of the home of the host, an important lawyer. The long discussion that ensued in this jasmine-scented enclosure developed into a gradual unfolding of secret Hindu beliefs that sent shivers of delight through the former Sanskrit scholar of the Sorbonne. It was this she had come, to see, touch, and feel. They explained to her that she merited these revelations because they could read in her eyes that she was an adept of raja yoga, going so far as to divulge in detail the arrangement of the innermost chamber of the temple. It seemed that, after traversing a room filled with many grimacing idols, one arrived at the "dwelling place of the god," hidden by a veil. When this curtain was lifted, there was revealed a completely empty enclosure. In spite of the presence of multiple images in wood and bronze, the god himself remained invisible even to the eyes of the devoted.[6]

After describing this extraordinary meeting, she makes one of several references to that "quicksand" of the Orient in which had disappeared a number of unprepared Europeans. On more than one occasion she seemed aware of being on the verge of such an experience herself. Her innate skepticism, however, served to maintain her stability.

Although her hospitable friend, Narusa, invited her to remain as a guest in his home, it was unthinkable, both because of the lack of sanitation and elementary hygiene, and her inability to digest the highly seasoned Indian cuisine. She declined as politely as possible. As an alternative she sought out the enclave of the Theosophical

Society, which had established its headquarters in Madras. When she and her Brahman friend arrived to inspect the place, they found the large garden full of figures in flowing garments "floating" in ethereal fashion about the premises. Narusa was much amused, but agreed with her that, even if it did resemble a lunatic asylum, she would be quite comfortable. This was indeed the case, though the mixture of Far Eastern and Louis XVI atmosphere created by the Theosophists struck her as humorous.[7]

Narusa was aware of her strong desire to experience "modern" Buddhism, which was beginning to infiltrate India in spite of Hindu and Moslem opposition. Since 1891 the Maha Bodhi Society, founded by Anagarika Dharmapala of Ceylon, had made a concerted effort to bring Buddhism back to the land of its origin. Narusa took her into a poor quarter to see what he referred to as Buddhist "evangelism." A leader of sorts explained something about Buddhist belief, after which there was a brief ceremony, followed by a discussion of the evolution of the animal species. The group of listeners, seated on the floor on mats, were "very attentive, very honest." Those Hindus who became Christian or Buddhist lost their caste and became pariahs. Alexandra had made friends with a Jewish woman converted to Buddhist belief who was about to leave India. She gave Alexandra some money with which to provide a festival for these poor people the day of the next full moon. Alexandra planned this with enthusiasm. Among other delights she could provide exotic illuminations and delicious native pastries. "That won't ruin my multimillionaire coreligionaire."[8]

Pondicherry, like Versailles, was a place that had once known grandeur, but had fallen into a condition of semidecay. After a long day of exploration, she went to interview Sri Aurobindo Ghose at his home. Sri Aurobindo, a revolutionary patriot of whom the British colonial government was very suspicious, had resided in

Pondicherry for only a short time. Born in 1872, he was sent by his family to study in England at the age of seven, and he remained there for fourteen years, completing his studies at Cambridge. After his return he was attached to the College of Baroda, but his journalistic and revolutionary activities resulted in his being condemned and imprisoned by the British at Alipore. Liberated in 1910, he immediately sought refuge in French territory at Pondicherry. Alexandra found him to possess a rare intelligence and lucidity. During the interview he was seated in front of a window through which appeared only the luminous green sky of India. Because his political opinions did not please the British, she discovered on her return to Adyar that the chief of security was waiting to interrogate her about her visit. She told him the truth, that their conversation had not even touched on politics. A few days later, seated next to the governor of Madras at a luncheon party in her honor, she found herself again subjected to questioning, and was characteristically annoyed by this intrusion on her privacy.

She often seemed to relish laughter at her own expense. During an excursion to the Seven Pagodas, she was on her way to discreetly brush her teeth in the garden of the bungalow where she was staying with friends, when she missed the steps in the dark and somersaulted into a potted shrub, landing on her back on the ground. She shrieked with pain and called for help, only to be struck full in the face, as the companion who was coming to her aid made the same mistake. When further assistance arrived, they found her doubled up with laughter at the comic scene.[9]

Toward the end of December in Adyar, she had a surprising visit by three Visnuites (adorers of Vishnu). Their faces were decorated with what she could clearly identify as "that sacred substance the cows emit naturally." They had come to make the astonishing proposal that she join their ranks: become a true yogi, living naked under a tree, devoting her life to the attainment of enlightenment. She explained as delicately as possible that on another continent she had a husband who would react with little enthusiasm to such a proposal. This discussion lasted over three hours, during which the men did their best to persuade her, speaking all at the same time, and enunciating with great emotion numerous Sanskrit texts, resounding in the large room like a fanfare from another age.[10]

Although she was deeply moved and impressed by the fervor of the devotees with whom she daily conversed, she clung to her Buddhist conviction that one should concern oneself with everyday realities and the alleviation of human suffering, rather than metaphysical speculation. It was indeed a period of adjustment for Alexandra. Her mind and her senses were being assaulted by repeated sequences of contrast and paradox. The artist in her was almost overwhelmed by the sights and sounds that pressed, one upon another, and inspired passages of such poetic beauty that translation becomes difficult. At the same time she was repeatedly horrified by the presence of filth and decay, and the "injustice," as she saw it, of Hindu life. She was finding it difficult to settle in, feeling herself equally out of place among the British colonials and the indigenous upper class. It was as though all her previous life, her beliefs, her assumptions, were being put to the test. From Calcutta she wrote about the mentality of the greater number of Vedantists, finding them deplorable, antihuman, and antisocial. She was not surprised that they had led India to such a miserable state. The reality she found was brutal, egotistical, contemptuous of human life, and inexpressibly filthy. Alexandra felt that anyone who had not witnessed the way in which the Hindus treated each other among different castes, and observed themselves the life of the "untouchables" should not speak of India.[11]

The father who bore on his shoulders a child of two years to see the massacre of the federals would surely have applauded such sentiments. They did not stand in the way of further discoveries, however.

"January 1, 1912 . . . Began the year in the waiting room of Kurda Road, the junction for Puri, where I set up my bed for a few hours. I had forgotten it was New Year's Eve. The surroundings were rather sinister, and I felt myself far away (from what?) and very much alone. Are not these times of anguish the antechamber of that great serenity which surpasses everything?"[12]

She was beginning to experience the multiple layers of meaning inherent in everything that surrounded her. The effect of this on her writing was a growing substance and dimension. Physical exhaustion was a constant menace. Her days were so full, and she continued to have difficulty digesting the Indian food. At times she missed Mouchy very much. She spoke of that most difficult moment when, sitting down alone at her small table for dinner, she looked about at the couples in evening dress seated nearby, and imagined how she would welcome the sight of her Mouchy in his handsome dinner jacket seated opposite her.

Another influence on her mode of expression was photography. She was becoming increasingly adept with her camera, and this was reflected in her written descriptions. She began to register and record, with increasing speed and accuracy, the multitude of impressions she witnessed every day. Her writing assumed the character of a sequence of snapshots, with background, foreground, movement, and atmospheric conditions taken into account.

Facing the panorama of *ghats* (terraces) across the Ganges, after a long day of philosophic discussion with the swamis at the *math* of Belur, she was captivated by the gentle hues of the approaching twilight. Rose and pale mauve, descending on the pearl-gray river, evoked an almost unbearable melancholy. She pressed her departure. The young Indians charged with escorting her back to her lodgings were interested in what had brought her to visit the swamis. When she mentioned that she was a Buddhist they begged her to tell them more about Buddhism.

And as the boat slowly drifted with the current, they pressed closely together around her as she spoke of the teaching of the Lord Buddha twenty-five centuries ago, farther up on the same river where it flowed past Benares.[13]

What a far cry this was from the lectures she had given before the "universitaires" of Paris and Brussels. The armor of European intellectualism she had forged over so many years began to fall away as she confronted the contrasts that daily assaulted her. At Durbar, also on the Ganges, she visited a celebrated temple of Kali, where she had to lift her skirt calf-high as she waded through the sea of blood from animal sacrifices. On another occasion at Durbar she delighted like an excited child when a parade of over sixty magnificently caparisoned elephants and camels passed in solemn line. Later in the day the animals returned, unadorned except for their painted foreheads and trunks. The majestic gray masses trudged slowly in the dust that, mingled with the mist of evening, revealed a procession out of time, beyond the reaches of civilization. It was a vision of solemnity and enduring beauty.

Calcutta was an enormous city divided into two parts, only the European section being habitable by her standards. She commented that it was just like being in London, with parks and elegant shops, but the Ganges instead of the Thames. But there was the omnipresent irritation of what she perceived as the hardness and brutality of the Hindus, their lack of charity and consideration for human life. The rigidity of the caste system amused and infuriated her by turns: the fact that one man could bring fruit to the table, or tea, and that the food that had been cooked must be delivered by another, of a different caste. There were the joys as well, to which she responded with enthusiasm. Her need for consistency began gradually to crumble. Plunging into the depths of another culture required discarding so many long-cherished assumptions. Every day produced a new revelation.

"Calcutta, January 13, 1912—What is Shiva in Paris—even at the Musée Guimet? A name? Yesterday it was the living symbol of a living thing."[14]

The continual confrontation of those opposites, life and death, occupied her mind and filled her imagination. Again she returned to the math of Belur for a celebration. She delighted in the exotic profusion of flowers, and the choir of young people who chanted hymns, scanning the measures with little silver bells. She was not only the sole European, but the only woman who had been invited to attend this important occasion. In the late afternoon she departed in a small boat to visit a temple. She was reliving the events of the day when her reverie was disturbed by a strange sight along the nearby shore. A dog was dragging a long red object it was trying to devour. She realized suddenly that the "object" was a cadaver, the head unrecognizable except for the rows of protruding teeth. The flesh was the consistency of leather, and the feet had been bound together. Since it was strictly forbidden to throw uncremated bodies into the river, she wondered if in fact the man had been a cadaver when he joined the current. She made an attempt to photograph the macabre scene.

Because of her linguistic facility Alexandra did not require an interpreter and was able to speak directly with people. This was an enormous advantage. Her skill as an interlocutor made for a relaxed exchange of ideas. An interview had been arranged for her with the widow of Sri Ramakrishna. This serenely elegant woman of over sixty was an extraordinary beauty. Their discussion touched on many things, among which was the condition of women in India. Afterward Alexandra was invited to visit a school for Hindu widows that an American woman had established. Since marriages were arranged for female infants still in the cradle, there were often widows as young as five years of age. Forbidden to remarry, these young women often became impoverished and were forced to resort to prostitution to survive. In this school the women were trained in useful and lucrative skills that would allow them to earn a living. It seemed like a minuscule effort to stem the tide of female misery, but it was an indication that, very slowly, things were beginning to improve.

She was a frequent guest in the home of wealthy Hindus, an unusual opportunity for a European woman. These soirees often included performances by musicians of renown who had been engaged for the occasion. Music still represented a supreme delight for Alexandra. She loved especially to listen to the oriental tonalities, which were not always pleasing to Western ears. But this unremitting social life was beginning to pall. It was not for this that she had come. In her diary for February second, she notes that she had been invited to attend a garden party given by the maharajah Bahadur of Burdwam, but at the last minute had sent her regrets. She was overcome by an intense "lassitude of morale," of a great desire for "the other shore," the refuge of Brahma.

In a period of four months Alexandra had absorbed a multitude of contrasting and conflicting impressions. Her senses had been continually assaulted, her emotional circuits repeatedly overloaded. On one hand she was treated to the exotic delights accessible only to those possessing wealth and power. But this perfumed veil did not conceal from her republican sensibilities the filth and misery in which the lower castes lived. To a fastidious woman with refined tastes the odors of blood, excrement, and unwashed human bodies must have been difficult to tolerate. She had immersed herself in a philosophic tradition that accommodated many contrasts, but her socialist convictions were often stretched to the limit.

Nevertheless, she possessed such an aura of authenticity that she was received with cordiality and respect by even the most erudite and sophisticated Brahmans. The simple people flocked to her, listened attentively to her expositions of Buddhist teaching, and requested her benediction. In this land where reincarnation was not considered merely a concept but a living reality, it was simply assumed that she had returned to the place where she had lived previously to continue an interrupted mission.

But the fragility of her digestive system began to betray her. She was very tired. The time had come to move on to Sikkim.

6

Sikkim the Incomparable

«April to October 1912»

The spring of 1912 was an exceptional time for Alexandra. Within a brief period there converged a trinity of personalities that would change the course of her life and influence the structure of her thought. First to arrive on the scene was the maharajah of Sikkim, Sidkeong Tulku, then His Holiness, the "Great" thirteenth Dalai Lama; finally, most important of all, the *gomchen* of Lachen, her Dharma master. He was the only person during her long lifetime who demanded and received absolute submission from Alexandra. With his help she completed the armature of conviction, begun with Ecclesiastes and the maxims of Epictetus, which would sustain her to the very end. Only an individual possessing extraordinary physical and intellectual endurance could have supported this density of experience. In April she wrote her "bien cher Mouchy," that as she left in the pale and luminous light of dawn, mounted upon her horse, she thought of Don Quixote departing for his adventures. Instead of a lance she carried a branch taken from a small bush by her groom, and she hoped that the "windmills" as well would be of modest proportion.[1]

The dense fog through which they moved contributed to the mystery of the departure from Lopchoo, their first halt on the route from Calcutta to Sikkim. Clouds drifting through the forest transformed the trees into ghostly giants. As always, she was sensitive to the presence of "her" trees. Proceeding at the head of a long column of servants and bearers, she threaded her way through the dense forest. Here at last, the flight in the Bois de Vincennes achieved its ultimate expression. Her awareness of the significance of this pilgrimage is suggested in her letter of April fourteenth, from Kalimpong, in which she spoke of "following the Star." But she was on her way to see a twenty-seven-year-old sovereign in exile, not the Christ in his creche.[2]

In Kalimpong, she was delighted with her accommodations. She was housed in a lovely bungalow, the larger part of which had been reserved for the young maharajah and his entourage, already in residence. The bedroom was large, high ceilinged and very clean—a condition, rare in the Orient, that she always noted with great satisfaction. Dividing the enormous bathroom in half with the waterproof in which her bed was wrapped, she created a kitchen. Finding adequate servants was a continuing problem, especially to do the cooking she required. For some time she had been a rigid vegetarian. This was in part a matter of conviction, in part because she was plagued throughout her life by digestive problems that were aggravated by meat.

Presented with the card of the young prince, who was eager to meet her, she availed herself of this invitation to go at once to see him. She described her initial impression to Mouchy.

"This Maharajah Kumar, Sidkeong Tulku, is the son of the real maharajah. He is a young man, very agreeable, and appears to be extremely intelligent. He was magnificently dressed in gold brocade."[3]

Within the subconscious of almost every woman, however independent and emancipated, however indifferent to the lure of romance, there lies buried a Sleeping Beauty who waits to be awakened. Alexandra was no exception. She was an artist who had evoked with feeling the great moments of the operatic repertoire. How appropriate that when her prince finally arrived on stage, he should be fitted out in gold brocade! The friendship that blossomed between this Eastern prince and a Western woman would have been unique in any era, but especially so in the early twentieth century, when European colonials maintained a certain distance from the "natives," no matter how high born. Sidkeong Tulku had received an excellent European education, and had graduated from Oxford. He had also spent eight years of his youth studying with a lama-precept, and was the titular head of the prevailing Buddhist sect of Sikkim, the Kaghu, referred to as the "Red Lamas." Alexandra ultimately became his confidante, his traveling companion, his spiritual sister. We have, as evidence of the nature of their relationship, not only her letters to her husband, but many letters written in English from Sidkeong to Alexandra. Since she considered herself dedicated to a religious vocation, and therefore celibate, and since he commanded the usual entourage of concubines available to an oriental prince, it is unlikely that the nature of this friendship was other than platonic. His letters were always addressed to "Dear Sister David-Néel." He believed from the beginning that, closely associated in a previous life, they had chosen to continue their work together.

Alexandra's reason for coming to Kalimpong was to see the exiled Dalai Lama, with whom she had obtained an audience for April 15, 1912. His Holiness was residing in Kalimpong, under the protection of the British government. The Manchu empire had invaded his country and were in complete control in Lhasa. He remained in Sikkim from 1910 until 1912, when the fall of the Manchu empire put a temporary end to Chinese domination. Alexandra was the first occidental woman he had agreed to receive, a singular honor, and there were complicated issues of protocol and behavior. It had been decided that she must wear an oriental robe, rather than European dress. This was to discourage other European women from following her example. Few European women would demean themselves to the extent of wearing a "native" costume. But Alexandra, during her stay in India, had begun to wear the long orange robe that identified her as a religious seeker. She had been well prepared for this audience by the good sisters of the Bois Fleuri, having rehearsed her "reverence" before the king and queen of Belgium. Wearing her "dawn-colored" robe and a salmon-colored veil (far more flattering, she noted, than the black required in Rome), she was carried to the Dalai Lama's residence in a sedan chair through dense fog and intermittent rain.

At a turning of the route she was surprised to see a small Mongolian shrine, vividly painted in red, blue, and gold, protecting a bust of the late Queen Victoria. As they continued, her thoughts turned suddenly to her father. She remembered with nostalgia their long walks together through the streets of Brussels, their many conversations, and realized how with age (she was then forty-five) she fully appreciated his exceptional intelligence. Whatever aspect of the somber procession allowed this memory to emerge, it revealed a rare moment of tenderness. Within the intrepid adventurer there existed still a "Nini" who had strolled the boulevards of Brussels, her hand firmly held by a tall, aristocratic man with whom she could discuss what was closest to her heart. She wished that he would appear, suddenly where the route turned, so that she could embrace him, this man who had created her entirely of his blood, without her mother having given her anything of herself.[4] It was the first of a number of significant turns in the route, and of encounters, not out of the past, but vividly in the present.

She descended from her chair (one was supposed to approach His Holiness's residence on foot), and saw a long avenue marked with tall poles carrying Tibetan pennants. The door of the modest chalet of the ruler in exile was guarded by two quite ordinary policemen ("*pauvre garde d'honneur!*"), and she, somewhat disappointed, noted with distaste that the chamberlain who admitted her was quite unclean. The interior of the building, though simple, met her exacting standards, however, and she did not have long to wait. Two Japanese gentlemen were received before her and speedily dismissed. It may well have been that His Holiness's curiosity was as keen as her own. When, bearing the long white scarf one traditionally presents to an important person in the East, she was ushered into his presence, she was quite overcome to find him seated, not on a throne, but in an ordinary chair beside the window. She recognized him from a photograph she had previously seen, but for once the "reporter" in her was inactive. She did not even notice his costume, though one can assume he was well turned out. In her excitement she completely forgot about the benediction, until reminded in a whisper by her Tibetan sponsor, Laden-La. Freethinking, independent, Protestant, and Freemason that she was, she could happily have dispensed with this required ritual, but she nevertheless complied, and bowed her head. He asked the same question many others had posed. How had she become a Buddhist? It was inconceivable to him that one could become a Buddhist on the bench of a European university by means of studying oriental philosophy and language.

But she explained to him that when she had adopted the principles of Buddhism she was perhaps the only Buddhist in Paris. He laughed and said that was, in effect, an excellent reason for having gone without an instructor.[5]

She noted that he was cheerful by nature, and admitted that he was "not an imbecile." Alexandra knew how to flatter, and she was always gifted at saying the right thing when it was required to obtain her goal. She gave as the reason for requesting this audience the hope that the "chief of northern Buddhism" (a slight exaggeration, but appreciated nonetheless) would elucidate for her certain questions to the end that this school of Buddhism might be better understood in Europe. It was finally decided that she would present her questions in writing, which would then be translated into Tibetan, that he might give his replies in writing. This was beyond her greatest hopes.[6] The audience lasted forty-five minutes. Then she executed a faultless exit, stepping backward toward the door (happy that the room was essentially unfurnished), and made a final bow.

The young maharajah was waiting for her at the bungalow. Having been educated in Europe, he was understandably curious about this encounter between a Western woman and the Dalai Lama. He exclaimed that if only he were the Dalai Lama he would make every effort to reform Buddhism, but Alexandra wisely replied that if he were the Dalai Lama he would not have traveled and seen all that he had seen, nor studied as he had, and that he would think exactly as did His Holiness.

On April twenty-second, after a brief tour near the Tibetan border, which the British had refused permission for her to cross,[7] she arrived in Gangtok, the capital of Sikkim. She was invited to the home of the maharajah for tea. Alexandra was delighted with the interior of his home, tastefully decorated in the European style. His inherited inclinations were evident, however, in the magnificent collection of Asian objets d'art he had brought back from his travels in Japan and China. She wrote to Mouchy of a beautiful ivory Buddha enclosed in a stained-glass shrine that she would love to have in their home. She spoke at length of the conversation she had over the tea cups on this occasion with a very learned lama invited to meet her. With the prince serving as interpreter, she was able to satisfy her curiosity concerning the lama's interpretation of such Western concepts as the existence of God and the soul.

Alexandra found such dialogues illuminating, but the silent vastness of the mountains beckoned irresistibly. She was soon on the move again, camping in the Himalayas with a few retainers and a minimum of equipment. The Tibetan plateau continued to tempt her to further exploration, to represent her ultimate desire. She discovered a crevice where a torrent exploded among the remnants of enormous trees, which looked to her like a scene of silent carnage, a battlefield of beings from another realm.[8] She was experiencing an identification with the natural world, above all its mysterious light, that transported her into this poetic mode of expression. It amounted to a kind of intoxication. She could not get enough, it would seem, and kept returning to the vast, empty regions. It was quite possibly the projection of that "inner landscape" that was evolving in this place. The "space" within her was expanding, and she was being drawn toward a new spiritual horizon. Her state of health improved enormously above a certain altitude, and all her problems of digestion and "neurasthenia" vanished. It would seem to explain the prodigious feats of which she was capable, the long hikes, the ability to survive on a diet that was marginal at best, and to withstand incredible extremes of temperature. She belonged in this place, and her body responded by an incredible rejuvenation. She could hardly recognize herself in the mirror. Many years had disappeared from her features, and she saw in her eyes a clarity that seemed to reflect the light of the mountains. Light was more than a metaphor, it was the physical context of her new awareness. She was poised on the threshold of a new life. There were lapses, of course. She was still the prey of petty vexations. The English newspaper had printed erroneously that she had "prostrated" herself before the Dalai Lama, and she was furious. She was as unforgiving as ever of the weaknesses of ordinary mortals. But her affection for Mouchy remained undiminished. "You see how much pleasure it gives me to write to you and recount the incidents of my voyage. That should prove to you, dearest, that although I find great pleasure in my travels, I do not forget you, and I will be happy to rejoin you at the end of my voyage."⁹

But after she had seen a mass of begonias enveloped by dazzling sunlight and the miraculous fluttering wings of red and blue birds and giant butterflies in flight she wondered how she could possibly return to "civilization," the agitation of mortal affairs, and a preoccupation with mundane considerations.

In Sikkim at this time there was a Swedish mission, directed by a Protestant pastor, Mr. Owen. The activities of this group were a constant source of amusement to Alexandra. Returning from one of her excursions on horseback, she paused at the mission to pay her respects and, since it was Pentecost, was invited to share their festive luncheon. She described the scene as resembling a barnyard with a flock of overfed hens clustered about the single (and singular) rooster, Mr. Owen. Since she did not carry a change of clothes with her when camping, she donned her orange Buddhist robe over the trousers she wore when riding. This created a modest sensation. After lunch Mr. Owen delivered a sermon on the devil, a favorite subject of the missionaries. Invited to express her opinion, Alexandra shocked them by saying she considered the devil a brother along with all other creatures, and she hoped he would eventually attain enlightenment.

That evening, returning to her quarters on horseback, between ranges of snow-covered peaks illuminated by a full moon, she was reminded of a painting she had seen of the adoration of Shiva in the mountains. "It was the light falling on the evergreens, the same mysterious illumination covering everything, the same invisible presence, the same silent voices chanting an inexpressible hymn."¹⁰

During another encounter with the missionaries, the subject under discussion was the recent sinking of the Titanic. It was the conviction of the good ladies that the passengers were sent to a watery grave as punishment because they were dancing and enjoying themselves on this "sinful pleasure voyage." After listening to this discussion she had a great desire to seek out the image of Chenresig that was enthroned on the altar of the local monastery. She longed to experience this many-headed, many-armed symbol of infinite compassion whose message proclaimed that there was no such thing as eternal perdition, that one could always emerge from despair. Though of little artistic significance, the rustic idol spoke eloquently of kindness and pity. Her experience of Buddhism was at last beginning to transcend art history. When she arrived at the monastery she did not enter immediately. The abbot, whom she had recently come to know, was waiting on the terrace to receive her, as though anticipating her arrival. The gomchen of Lachen had made his entrance into her life.

There is a saying that when the moment is right, the teacher will appear. Alexandra herself makes some interesting comments about the role of the guru in her book *L'Inde où j'ai vécu*,[11] remarking that within the Hindu tradition the intrinsic worth of the guru is of little importance. From the point of view of contemporary morality, the man may be vulgar or even reprehensible. What is important is the sentiment the guru awakens in the believer, and whether or not he has the power to evoke those energies that otherwise would remain dormant. She maintained therefore, that it is better to leave to the guru his conventions, and not to investigate too carefully his intelligence or his erudition, because the benefit comes from the fervor of the disciple, and the mental and physical transformation that makes of him a totally new person. She explains this attitude in the context of Tibetan Buddhism in a footnote in the same volume.[12] Since the Buddhists deny the existence of an ego that is separate, and see the individual as a succession of changing aggregates moving along in the manner of a stream of energy, the intelligent disciple supports the inferior manifestations of the guru in the same way that he might wait patiently in a vulgar crowd for the passing of a sage. One has the distinct impression that these words were inspired not only by her keen observation of Hindu and Buddhist practices, but by her own experience as well. Although she and the gomchen belonged to different worlds, she felt that when they discussed philosophy, they essentially shared the same ideas and hopes, even though under very different terms, and dreamed the same dreams.[13]

After Alexandra had absorbed the benefits of Sanskrit studies, had received instruction from teachers in India, and had experienced the eloquent silence of the mountainous expanses of Sikkim, she was ready to encounter a true master. After their first encounter, Alexandra was invited to visit the gomchen in his private chapel in the company of the reverend Owen, who was to serve as interpreter. On the altar of the chapel were enthroned the figures of Chenresig, the Buddha, and Padmasambhava, the great apostle of Tibet. The walls were covered with frescoes representing symbolic divinities in their most frightening aspects, the purpose of which was to remind the initiates of the cyclic activity of existence, destruction producing life, which in turn becomes dissolution, decay, and death. The only light entered by means of a small stained-glass window. The gomchen was seated in the lotus position on a pile of carpets. He was tall and thin, his hair arranged in a long braid that reached to his heels. He was dressed in a red and yellow costume quite different from that worn by the lamas of Sikkim. His face reflected his intelligence, his assurance, and the special illumination characteristic of those who had for many years been adepts of yogic practice. Mr. Owen did his best to follow the commentary of the gomchen, but frequently floundered. In spite of this, Alexandra and the gomchen understood each other in a deep sense. She received confirmation of her theories of the penetration of the Vedanta into northern Buddhism, and other concepts that had evolved from her Sanskrit studies. During this period a movement of reform had penetrated Sikkim, and the maharajah and the gomchen were both making an effort to purify Buddhism from the accretions of superstition, folklore, and magic that weighed heavily on the original teaching of the Buddha.

It was grand and impressive for her to see the yogi sweep the assembled images and symbols with a wide gesture of repudiation, declaring that they were only good for people with little intelligence. He then resumed the thought of the Upanishads, the principal philosophy of India—"Find all within yourself." The lama asked her several questions and then told her that she had seen the ultimate and supreme light. Throughout the conversation, the poor reverend translated without understanding. "He was more a stranger to our dialogue than the wooden pillars in front of us."[14]

It is tempting to speculate on the motives of these three men who were willing to devote themselves to teaching "La Parisienne." His Holiness, "no imbecile" by Alexandra's exacting standards, was well aware of what the future might hold for his country. He did not need to resort to clairvoyance or magic to see the large appetites of his greedy neighbors. In this remote and isolated part of the world, where omens and oracles were considered a mode of scientific investigation, did they see in her the future of Buddhism? Did they find her, gifted in linguistic skills, understanding and, above all, fervor, a possible instrument for communicating with the West? And did they succeed in conveying to her a sense of historic mission?

When one considers the position of women in the Orient at this time, sequestered, enslaved, illiterate and mute, it is nothing less than astounding that she was able to command, not only their attention, but their respect. Instead of rejecting her as pretentious and extravagant, they appreciated the sharp intelligence that she brought to these encounters. She made it clear that she had come with one desire only—to listen and to learn. With their sympathetic guidance she grew in wisdom and insight. The egocentric "diva," the audacious adventurer evolved gradually into a dedicated seeker. Alexandra's route would be long, with many digressions. The Tibetan Buddhists conceive of "illumination" not as the sudden flash of understanding characteristic of Zen, but as a long process of evolution comprising many years and even many lifetimes. Well versed in the literature and diverse methods of many Hindu and Buddhist traditions, Alexandra did not enter into this engagement lightly. She knew at the outset that following the Path involved a life-long commitment. She abhorred the nonchalance and dilettantism that characterized many Westerners seduced by Eastern philosophy at this time. Her mentors were astute enough to recognize this fact.

The weeks in Sikkim, passing in colorful procession, rivaled the most outrageous imaginings of Verdi. Dressed in her flowing orange robe, Alexandra joined the maharajah in stately processions. One spectacle was succeeded immediately by another. Following these impressive ceremonies, Sidkeong, Alexandra, and the gomchen retired into the latter's private quarters for intimate conversations and discussions of Buddhist texts. The young prince treated her with solicitude and deference. One of his letters demonstrates his very real respect: "Dear Sister David-Neél—There is no doubt that we must have wished in our previous life that we should meet here, and discuss on religious subjects. As you say, when we have got this grand opportunity we should try and devote ourselves in finding the real truth. I shall be very grateful to you if you will kindly give me a note about the way of meditation, and a formula of daily ritual for the use of the monasteries in Sikkim."[15]

In a cloud of incense, Alexandra walked between rows of prostrate subjects, followed by the young prince, who made certain she was always seated opposite him on the dais in the temples they visited. There she would be invited to deliver discourses on the subject of Buddhist

reform. The very fact that she must have seemed to the
indigenous assembly like a visitor from another planet
made it possible for her to make statements that otherwise would have been interpreted as sheer heresy. It is
important to remember also that the Tibetan cosmology
included female magicians and incarnations possessing
extraordinary psychic powers. Her sudden appearance
was undoubtedly interpreted in this context. Sidkeong's
efforts to implement numerous reforms suddenly received support from a source he could not have imagined
in his wildest dreams. That she appeared to him as a gift
from the gods was in no way an exaggeration. It is not
surprising that she was listened to with great seriousness
and venerated as an exceptional being.

And Mouchy must have reacted with a mixture of awe
and stupefaction as she recounted the gomchen presenting her with the white scarf that had been ritually
returned to him by the maharajah as they departed on
an expedition into the mountains. As he performed this
gesture of benediction and homage, the gomchen praised
her wisdom concerning the urgent need for reform, and
promised to send translations of her ideas to his colleagues in Tibet. "For the moment I rest enchanted. I
have been on the brink of a mystery! . . . The true Tibet,
terrifying and alluring, that I contemplated. Yes, I will
go on dreaming a long time—all my life—and a bond
will remain between me and this country of clouds and
snow, because my thoughts, translated and printed in
Tibetan, will travel who knows where across the country."[16]

These excursions were often true tests of endurance
for Alexandra. Once she narrowly escaped death by
suffocation when a sudden heavy snowfall collapsed her
tent. On another occasion a baby bear that was paraded
on a leash by the prince's retainers was quartered in an
adjacent room and whimpered pitifully during the night.
At three A.M., having finally fallen asleep, she was again
disturbed when the orchestra that accompanied the ma-

harajah wherever he traveled began to play a merry tune. At five A.M. the entourage began to prepare for its departure and, in spite of her fatigue, she arose to witness the event. (She and her escort were to follow later in the morning.) To her tired eyes there was revealed a scene rivaling in splendor a European tapestry of the Middle Ages, a weaving together of color, sound, and movement. The bodyguards surrounding the prince were dressed in red, and wore "Tyrolean" hats of bamboo, decorated with tall, swaying peacock feathers that lined up exactly with the slim carbines they carried. The maharajah appeared in a hooded cloak of gold brocade, mounted his horse, and with bearers, bodyguard, mounted attendants, and musicians (still playing vigorously), began to climb the steep slope under pouring rain, disappearing finally in the early morning mist that concealed the mountain peaks.

Alexandra spoke often of dreaming. Unfortunately she did not record many of her actual dreams. But it would seem that the two worlds were merging, being assimilated as part of the process of metamorphosis that was taking place. For some at high altitudes the dream world becomes more vivid, more explicit, and the (so-called) real world possesses more the quality of a dream. One of these qualities is the compression of images, of awareness on many levels simultaneously. She was responding in a single moment to the extraordinary visual stimulation of colors, textures, and forms; to the "presence" of the natural world, the trees, mountains, and rushing rivers, the alternation of fog and sunlight; to the personalities with whom she was associating, and to the accumulated learning of centuries, the language, ideas, and concepts she was absorbing. It is not surprising that her prose becomes "heavier" and more concentrated. On August 19th she wrote that she had completed the introduction to her *Life of Milarepa*, and was very pleased with it, describing it as being in a "musical" style. There comes a time when speculation no longer seems of great importance, for one has tasted other things, opened another door. One then approaches the threshold where faith, hope, anxiety, and desire no longer exist. That, she felt, was the beginning of wisdom.[17]

She encountered the Dalai Lama once again, as he was returning to his country. The Chinese revolution, which resulted in a mutiny of the troops garrisoned in Lhasa, had brought his exile in India to a sudden, unanticipated end. On this triumphal occasion he was mounted on a splendid horse, and his moustache and goatee added to the impression that he was more like a musketeer than a pope.[18] He had the reputation of being an excellent horseman, riding at such a pace that it was difficult for his retainers to keep up with him. He invited Alexandra to come to him, and graciously offered to continue sending her answers to her questions through the British agent, Mr. Bell.[19] In spite of this she said she did not find him sympathetic. Undoubtedly it was difficult for one with her republican, antimonarchist background not to perceive him as a despotic ruler. But then, she saw herself fulfilling the role of a "protestant" reformer, come to purify Buddhism from the defilements of the centuries. The tradition of the Huguenots died hard, and flourished with transplanting. She did admit, however, that he was more intelligent philosophically than was realized in the West—an effort to be fair, while damning with faint praise. She told Mouchy that she would keep the white silk scarf he had presented to her as a "souvenir de voyage," but that it did not possess for her the meaning of that presented by the gomchen among the rhododendrons one morning when, for a moment at least, three very different spirits were joined in the same desire, the same aspiration. She treasured it as a relic, a remembrance of one of those rare and vibrant moments one can count in a lifetime.[20]

The evenings with Sidkeong followed a prescribed ritual. They dined together, after which sticks of incense were lighted, and Buddhist philosophy and reform en-

thusiastically discussed. On one occasion it seemed that
they lost themselves in the reading of the *Dhammapada*
until one o'clock in the morning. But for Alexandra, as
she wrote Mouchy, there was always something further
on; and it was toward the "further on" that she held out
her arms.[21]

With that sense of perfect timing that characterizes
the most gifted performers, Alexandra realized that soon
she must move on. One of her problems was the disapproval with which the colonials viewed her close ties to
the court. The two maharajahs were only too eager to
offer her the hospitality of their very comfortable quarters. But to the English it was unthinkable that a "lady"
would accept such an arrangement. She was diplomatic
enough to want to avoid a rift. Therefore she decided to
go on to Nepal, to make a long anticipated pilgrimage to
the land of the Buddha. Before leaving, however, she
agreed to make a last trip into the mountains to visit a
number of temples that were under the supervision of
the prince, to pursue her dream of Asia, which she
understood and where at last she was understood.[22]
Whether this was indeed true or not, the important thing
was her feeling that at last she was understood, and was
not considered an anomaly to be avoided. Her opinions
did not have to be explained, much less justified. As they
left for the mountains there was the usual ritual of
departure. After traveling six hours without a halt, they
were greeted by a party of lamas who had come out to
meet them. Before a background of towering snow-
covered peaks stood a formation of garnet-clad lamas.
There were the usual multiple prostrations and offerings. The young prince, often boyishly exuberant and
ready for jokes and pranks, responded with great solemnity. "My young friend, for whom I have a great deal of
affection, is often very entertaining. It is a pleasure to
see this little man, as small as a Japanese, mounted on
his horse, receive gravely the scarves which the tall,
vigorous lamas give him and pass them around their

necks as a sign of benediction. The benediction of an 'incarnation' is infinitely precious."[23]

The spacious room reserved for her was decorated with a magnificent blue carpet and silk-embroidered "throws," but only torn paper covered the large windows. An open balcony served as bathroom. She dined with Sidkeong who, as abbot of the monastery, resided in a magnificent chamber with an altar. After dinner they discussed their favorite subject of reform to the sometimes deafening accompaniment of monks chanting in the chapel below. On the altar, the figure of Padmasambhava, illuminated by silver lamps, seemed to defy their attack on his creation. Sleep did not come easily to her, stretched out on her camping cot in the center of the enormous room that resembled an exotic stage setting. The light of the full moon penetrated the torn paper windows and shed an unearthly glow over the blue carpet and the silk coverings. The following morning she delivered her discourse seated on a leopard skin before the long rows of attentive lamas. Later they made a difficult climb to an even higher chapel where Sidkeong had spent much of his solitary youth. After the death of his mother he was more or less banished to this place, while his father reserved all his solicitude for a younger brother, the son of his second wife. Although Sidkeong continued to insist on his position as the rightful heir-apparent, the rift was never healed, and there was bad feeling between the two maharajahs. As they descended from this solitary temple their way was made very difficult by the flowing torrents of water that had swept away much of the route, and the constant presence of leeches that clung to their ankles and feet. Arriving at still another temple they feasted on grilled corn and fruits served on banana leaves, after which young monks danced the "skeleton dance" for the prince. Alexandra was quite transported by the surrounding snow-covered mountains, illuminated by a full moon, and the magical interior of the temple where altar lights danced on the figure of the immense Buddha presiding on the altar. It was unquestionably one of those precious hours to enclose in the reliquary of memories of beauty, art, and poetry.[24]

Once again sleep defied her. She was plagued by hordes of mosquitoes, by the hairpins that scraped her scalp, and by the discomfort of her stockings stiffened by the mud through which she had tramped. There are photographs of the intrepid adventurer on this occasion, showing her in a long dress, more appropriate for a shopping expedition on the Champs-Elysées than for mountain climbing. For some reason she had abandoned her usual trousers.

After an interminable descent they were finally met by their servants with horses, and the rest of the return was less arduous. There was another pause, however, where the prince had arranged for them to be served a proper English tea with toast and marmalade, a habit acquired during his student years in Oxford. They had returned to civilization.

Mouchy was getting restless, beginning to insist on her return. Although referring with nostalgia to their beautiful home in Tunis and Sophie's superb cuisine, she repeated her plans for continued studies, and wrapped it up succinctly, telling him that returning immediately was out of the question, for it did not seem desirable to her.[25]

She does go so far as to predict, however, that this would be her last voyage. It was the beginning of endless exchanges between them devoted to the same theme. Alexandra always prevailed. Philippe always shrugged his shoulders (he was perhaps more of a philosopher than she realized), and arranged for another bank draft.

7

Paradise Lost

«1912-1913»

The night was so dark that she could see nothing at all ahead of her, not even the white horse of the prince, which she knew was so close that their two beasts touched each other. As the procession wound its way through the ghostly trees of the forest and began the long descent to Darjeeling, Sidkeong began to chant a hymn composed by Milarepa in honor of his guru. "Oh, precious Guru, I see you seated on the lotus which is in the center of my heart." A few of the others picked up the chant and so, enveloped in darkness, they continued down, and down.

Alexandra emerged from her deep reverie with a sudden start, realizing that they had reached the end of their descent. The first electric light appeared. In the far distance the villas and hotels of the city shone in the night. It was the end of enchantment. The song of Milarepa had ceased. The flutes and drums that had so joyfully accompanied the long march from Gangtok were silent. The colorful procession that had advanced over passes and plateaus, and through the midnight forest emerged onto the wide avenue like the remnants of a carnival, pitiful and forlorn. All at once, Alexandra experienced the rancid taste of shame. The gods, the genies, the mountain spirits that had animated the cortege had fled. Abandoned and alone, she wakened from her dream, realizing with horror that in fact it was to this cold, electric world that she belonged. At a stroke her vision was eclipsed, and the harsh reality of "the civilized" reclaimed her. She was being delivered once again to all she had hoped to escape. Inside the luxurious room that had been reserved for her in Darjeeling's most elegant hotel, her one reaction was to burst into tears. She had forgotten the price required of all those who dare to ascend the heights—the inevitable descent.

But the prince whose solicitude had accompanied her return did not abandon her without a gesture of farewell. The following morning he presented himself, bearing in his hands not only the ritual scarf, but something of even greater significance. It was a delicate bronze Buddha that had been carried tenderly in the hands of the very first Karmapa lama to enter his country from Tibet. For centuries it had been venerated in one of the most important temples of Sikkim. The decision to remove it and send it to a distant land in the possession of a European woman could have been taken only after long and careful deliberation by the maharajah and his lamas.[1] In addition to this gift, he presented her with a length of heavy Chinese silk, deep gold in color, to wear over her shoulder as part of her religious apparel. But his ritualized adieu left Alexandra with something of even greater consequence. The validity and integrity of her mission had been restored to her.

She was forced to spend a short time in Calcutta completing preparations for her planned trip to Nepal. This abrupt immersion in British colonial life left her despairing and exhausted. The necessity of packing two complete wardrobes, one for exploring, and another for colonial social life, also irritated her. Six months of freedom from corsets had been delicious, but she could no longer fit into her evening wardrobe without painful lacings. She longed for a life that required only her religious robes. The months of isolation from the exigencies of colonial life, for study, rituals, and meditation had only increased her aversion to the demands of the world. But she was already forced to pay the price of being a celebrity, and was in constant demand to enliven the tedious existence of the colonials. Even the prospect of a lovely trip to Gaya and a bungalow across from the emperor Ashoka's temple did not lift her spirits. At last, on November twenty-third, she wrote from Kathmandu: "Once more I turn my back on Western civilization, joyously, with a feeling of relief, of repose, of being at last unburdened—the snow-capped peaks become rose in the light of the setting sun—the first sparkling star appears—the moment is so beautiful, calm, and blissful that one sinks into it, drowning gently, deeply, infinitely."[2]

However firmly she had turned her back on civilization, her adventure in Nepal could hardly be called "roughing it." The principal amusement in oriental courts was entertaining important guests. Having received numerous letters of introduction describing the unique attributes of this unusual visitor, the maharajah of Nepal was not to be outdone by his neighbor in Sikkim. And since Nepal was an independent state that "suffered" the British presence, the two factions were in strong competition to facilitate her voyage. "Facilitate" for the maharajah meant sending a magnificent horse-drawn landau, attended by servants wearing green and gold turbans; for the English it meant the constant presence of an orderly to see to all her needs. There were, in addition to a complete complement of servants, a guide, an interpreter, a saddle horse, and elephants as needed.

Her first outing was to the region where legend had located the Supreme Sacrifice, which had so intrigued her when she was a student at the Bois Fleuri. Alexandra had eagerly anticipated this excursion, but she found the region so civilized and cultivated, it was hard to imagine that a tigress had ever lived there. Nevertheless, she reveled in her camping deluxe provided by the maharajah, her enormous tent with carpets laid on beds of fragrant grasses, the servants attending to her every need. She made a tour of the entire area where presumably the Buddha had spent his youth, and tried to imagine what it must have been like in that remote time.

When she returned from this expedition an emissary of the maharajah of Nepal arrived with his gifts for her—an ornamental *kookri*, the traditional sword carried by Nepalese warriors, three sets of presentation coins in gold, silver, and copper, sets of stamps and postcards and other indigenous objects. This was considered a routine gesture for one of his importance. The giving and receiving of gifts was a ritual of enormous significance in this part of the world.

There were frequent letters from the court of Sikkim. On heavily embossed, crested stationery the prince shared with Alexandra his many problems, among them his vexation with the lamas who persisted in imbibing the local brew, and frequent misunderstandings with the Swedish mission. There were notes and texts from the Tashi Lama and other scholars, and a long epistle from a hermit of her acquaintance. Because of the translations of her recent writings on Buddhist reform that the gomchen had sent to colleagues in Tibet, her reputation had extended well beyond the frontier she herself was prevented from crossing. She was even rumored to be the incarnation of a *dakini*—a feminine deity. In another letter, Sidkeong assured her he would write a letter of introduction to the maharajah of Benares. The silken carpet would, thanks to his devotion, extend always before her on her travels. He reiterated his desire to become a Freemason. He and her faithful translator, Dawasandup, had kept their vows of temperance and continued with their meditations. He hoped very much to meet her in India.

On December 12, 1912, Alexandra wrote her husband at great length to wish him well for the New Year, and to say again how deep was her gratitude for all he had done for her. "Each day I find myself further from the illusions and agitations (of the world). A great repose, a great illumination enters into me, or rather, I enter into them. Nirvana is reality. . . . You have a wife who carries your name with dignity. If you were to pass where she has been, you would gather many compliments. With your support and aid I shall become an author of renown. . . . In our time, who would say something important must write it."[3]

Her welcome in Kathmandu was overwhelming. The British and Scotch Protestant residents vied for her presence during the Christmas holidays, not wanting her to be alone, which was the condition she most desired. She found the noise of conversation more and more disagreeable, and the effort of making "small talk" exhausting. She longed for solitude and silence, and wondered if she would ever again be able to tolerate a "civilized" life.

Early in January she left again with her well-loaded elephants to visit the sites of the Buddha's youth. Near Rumindei, the place of his birth according to tradition, she camped in a mango grove. It reminded her of the story of Ambapali, a beautiful courtesan who lived in just such a grove of mangos. This legendary woman was an intellectual and scholar who it was believed was visited by the Buddha. According to the legend, she and Visaka were the only women capable of understanding the profound and subtle doctrine. Ambapali became a disciple, giving up her life of ease, with no sense of expiation or guilt, but like a queen who has realized the vanity of her throne.[4] Needless to say, Alexandra was inspired by this story.

Soon thereafter Alexandra experienced one of the more colorful events of her entire life. Finding an especially delightful place to set up camp, she could not persuade the others to remain. They had heard rumors that man-eating tigers had been sighted in the vicinity. Nevertheless she decided to make a brief halt, going off to meditate under a large tree in a place she described as being "delicious." She sent her boy off with instructions to return in a few hours with her elephant, and

plunged immediately into a state of samadhi.[5] Her meditation was suddenly disturbed by the sound of leaves
crackling under the weight of heavy, cautious paws.
Annoyed at this intrusion, she opened her eyes. At a
distance of no more than twenty meters, she saw a long,
striped coat partly obscured by foliage, above which
could be seen two ears lifted on the alert. Her first
thought, a zebra! Then she recalled that zebras were not
to be found in that part of the world. Besides, the coat
was not black and white, but a deep reddish yellow
color, with black markings. It could only be a tiger. She
reflected, her heart pounding furiously, that if she
moved or made the slightest sound, he could reach her
in two leaps. She also remembered the tradition that
dictated that a *sannyasin*[6] never turned away from danger. Her best recourse was to remain immobile. Not
without difficulty, she again closed her eyes and resumed
her deep concentration. Some time later the thought
came to her that it had been a trick of perception. What
she had imagined to be a tiger could as easily have been
a mass of reddish leaves marked by shadows. She opened
her eyes. Where there had been "reddish leaves," she
saw only green foliage framing the evening sky. Her
elephant was waiting, and as they moved away she noticed a large pile of bones, a veritable ossuary. She had
chosen to meditate in the tiger's favorite eating place.

In spite of the luxurious attention provided by the
court, she was ready to leave Nepal. She found the
atmosphere of this small kingdom suffocating, too much
as she imagined Europe during the Middle Ages. At nine
each evening, for example, a cannon's roar announced
the beginning of the curfew, and the city was closed.
There were constant interruptions by well-meaning colonials. She felt a need for solitude and quiet once more,
for time to reflect on what she had experienced. As she
prepared to depart for Benares, she thought of the rose
garden of so long ago where an aging holy man had
whispered to her of impermanence.

As before, her arrival was preceded by many letters
of introduction. To make a spontaneous appearance
would not have been considered correct. The demands
of early-twentieth-century protocol were elaborate, especially in the Orient. Having received news of her
arrival from the court of Sikkim, the maharajah of
Benares lost no time in sending for such an "original"
visitor. Since his palace was located at some distance, he
sent a limousine to fetch her.

"The Maharajah is the most successful representation
of Offenbach one could imagine. He was dressed in violet
and gold, with a little gold toque on his head. I was
delighted just to contemplate him."[7]

The comedy was only beginning. A group of German
Rothschilds arrived soon after Alexandra. They were
"en tour," and the maharajah was part of their itinerary. They proved to be "even more Offenbach" than His
Highness, and it lacked only an orchestra to set everyone
singing and dancing with enthusiasm. The only sour note
in the performance was struck when the German visitors
admired the many magnificent European objets d'art,
and the somewhat flustered monarch replied that whenever he needed something truly elegant he was obliged to
send to France for it. This faux pas gave La Parisienne a
fit of giggles once she had regained the privacy of her
limousine.

Another amusing incident took place in the course of
a large Hindu banquet to which she had been invited.
On this occasion she managed to have several French
friends included, that they might experience something
outside the usual range of tourist attractions. Things
were going smoothly when a drama suddenly erupted. A
pious Brahman had discovered that he had inadvertently
seated himself beside a layman of lower caste, and had
actually eaten in his presence, a mortal error. There
followed much screaming and raving. Alexandra could
not resist sending a messenger to inform the two unfor-
tunates that, since "only Brahman exists" and "all is

Brahman," "Brahman had dined with Brahman" and, consequently, there could be no cause for regret. Her message was not greeted with mirth, but the brouhaha ceased.[8]

Benares attracted many European tourists who made a point of contacting Alexandra. As the celebrity of the moment, she found it difficult to refuse their invitations. The evenings when she was obliged to abandon her comfortable sari and be laced into the infamous corset to dine at the Hôtel de Paris were always painful. "Truly these people and their gestures seem to have escaped from an insane asylum. I ask myself 'which of us is crazy?' And the ironic reply arises from I don't know what interior tabernacle, 'Both of you!'"[9]

There were many exotic delights. She and her French friends watched the eclipse of the moon from a boat floating on the Ganges. Over one hundred thousand devotees had gathered on the terraces to bathe in the river as a ritual of propitiation. These ghats[10] were a major attraction in Benares. The burning ghats attracted the greatest curiosity among Western visitors. With an objectivity rare for a European woman she reported the cremation rites in minute and explicit detail. Frequently those in extremis were carried by their relatives to the cremation site, and for hours or even days were forced to endure the smell and sound of the rite that awaited them.

Music, the sounds and the structures of tonal accompaniments, formed a constant counterpoint to Indian festivals, for music was always present. These she often recorded with detailed notations indicating the rhythm and tonality involved. She was a frequent guest in the homes of wealthy music lovers, where concerts were presented for her enjoyment. On one such occasion she had been invited to hear a prominent singer in the salon of a wealthy Benares merchant. The artist, a beautiful young woman dressed in pale blue, was seated on white cushions between two candelabras. Before her, silver plates were arranged containing jasmine and rose petals, and silver dust. As she sang she gracefully sprinkled the dust over the petals, which servants then scattered on the heads of the assembly, leaving "diamonds" in their hair. All the guests were decorated with multiple garlands of flowers placed about their necks and on their arms. Alexandra described it as a feast of sight and sound.

But she had come to work, not to be entertained. Every day she arose very early, spent long hours in meditation, and then devoted herself to her Sanskrit studies, even though her professor of Sanskrit was so filthy she could hardly bear his presence. As the extreme heat of summer increased, her health declined. She was prey to severe colitis, which weakened her entire system. Nevertheless she wrote prolifically, continued her studies, and covered the entire city on foot, visiting the temples and the many sages who congregated in this ancient center. One whom she particularly revered was the Vedantist Satchitananda, who instructed her in the discipline of the Vedanta, about which she was writing a book. She traveled through the intense heat of the narrow, filthy streets to his tiny retreat. There, in an immaculately clean room, its only furnishings two chairs and his bedding rolled neatly in a corner, they sat, looking out over roofs and gardens toward the Ganges, discussing the tradition of the Vedanta. These were the hours she most cherished.

Alexandra could not bear to miss an opportunity to enlarge her understanding or increase her knowledge of any esoteric subject. She devoured every moment with relish, and neither fatigue nor illness stood in the way of a new contact or an original discovery. "Mad dogs, Englishmen, and Alexandra David-Néel" alone went out in the noonday sun of Benares. Her health might desert her, but never her sense of humor. One particularly hilarious day was spent in the company of a short, obese, Anglican clergyman (who had abandoned his clerics for a Sherlock Holmes check suit), a tall, thin, sparsely clad yogi, and a Tibetan lama. The four of them raced across the length and breadth of Benares, from sage to sage, from Hindu to Jain to whoever would receive them, sampling the varieties of philosophic delights for which the ancient city was famous.

Then, her mood suddenly changing, she would immerse herself in an exploration of the concept of renunciation as expressed in the *Bhagavad Gita,* increasing her sharply honed discernment and insight.

She wrote Mouchy that in return for what he had done for her, she longed to lead him to the wide-open door that she had discovered, but she feared he would not be interested.[11] Alexandra's absence of "a few months" had now been extended to two years. Not only was Mouchy not interested in following her through the open door she had discovered, but he accused her of having "married" the orange robe. Once again she explained that the robe constituted a refuge stronger than the walls of a convent—an asylum of peace, a defense against the insanity and egoism of the world. She reminded him of the painful years of neurasthenia she had suffered after their marriage. These voluminous explanations, justifications, and entreaties required hours of work on her part. Mouchy had informed her of his plans to retire. His income would be greatly curtailed, and he would be even lonelier without her. He pressed her to return as soon as possible. Without a doubt his pleas aggravated her digestive ailments. Her health continued to decline, her weight fluctuated wildly, her mental state became more and more unstable, her neurasthenia returned with a vengeance. The heat was unbelievably oppressive, and she dreamed of her beloved mountains.

There was good news from this direction, however. Her loyal and devoted "brother" Sidkeong saw to it that she was kept informed. He had even arranged to become a Freemason in Calcutta, which delighted her, as this forged another strong bond between them. He told her that their movement of reform was beginning to manifest itself in the monasteries among the more intelligent lamas. What they had initiated with such fervor was taking hold. A box of talismans arrived from Tibet, carried on the back of an aged lama who arrived in Benares on foot, to witness the esteem in which she was held in his country. This buoyed her spirits enormously. In spite of painful days and sleepless nights, she continued to write her books on India and the Vedanta. Her activity and her studies only accelerated. Her capacity for work, even under the most difficult conditions, was heroic.

Then she ceased to write. Beginning in September 1913, for an extended period there was silence; no further entreaties or explanations. Her pen was dry. There is no question that she was torn between her emotional commitment to Mouchy and the inner pressure to continue in the direction that drew her so insistently. She was searching for the solution that would satisfy both her needs, realizing the impossibility of moving in opposite directions. The silence was finally broken on December seventh in a letter postmarked Gangtok. The mountains had reclaimed her.

8

In the Ways of the Heart

«1913~1916»

Diary, November 28, 1913—"I leave tomorrow for Gangtok—and who knows where? This evening I made a little tour on horseback to look at the snow-capped mountains in the sunset. How enigmatic, how disquieting are the Himalayas this time. I do not understand. Why have I returned here? What will happen to me?"

The schoolchildren were the first to see her. For hours they had stood in quiet anticipation with their masters, watching the road intently for a first glimpse. When she came in view they moved forward, gravely bearing the white scarves of welcome, then fell in behind her retinue. Next she was greeted by a deputation of lamas, followed by rows of the high nobility and landowners, dressed as for a fete, all of whom joined the cortege. Then a very high-ranking lama, standing alone, bowed with great solemnity. Only Verdi could have done justice to the scene. At last she saw the prince. The sun shone on his gold-brocade tunic and awakened the sparkling diamonds on his toque. He moved forward, smiling, to offer her the scarf he owed only to his father and the Dalai Lama. She had come home.

The trip had not been an easy one. On the morning of her departure from Rungpo she had awakened with such severe rheumatic pain she wondered if she could even leave her bed. After enduring a long session of Scottish hydrotherapy, alternating very hot and very cold water, she managed to mount her horse for the strenuous, all-day journey to Gangtok.

After the intense heat of Benares, she suffered from the contrastingly cold climate of the mountains. There was a disappointment, as well. The voyage to Bhutan she had looked forward to making in the company of Sidkeong would be indefinitely postponed, due to the severe illness of his father. She moved into the residency of the British governor and began to endure colonial life—the evenings in dinner dress, the teas, the interminable games of "patience." After the months in Benares, corsetless and draped in filmy saris, she found European clothes impossibly restraining. After the long afternoons beside the Ganges in the company of Hindu sages, the tea party chit-chat of the colonials drove her nearly to distraction. And Sidkeong, on whose unwilling shoulders had fallen the responsibilities of government, was rarely available. She sent New Year's greetings to Mouchy on December 7, 1913: "On this day when many couples begin the New Year physically side by side, but widely separated in spirit, be sure that 'Moumi's' thoughts, filled with sincere affection, remain very close to you."[1]

For Alexandra, inactivity always resulted in depression. Soon after her arrival she was presented to a visiting Chinese Buddhist scholar at the palace. She spoke to him at length of her overriding concern, the degeneration of Buddhism. She posed the question: What good had it been, the preaching of the Buddha? What had he accomplished after all? The scholar's reply was very simple. He had given peace to them and to many others.[2]

His answer did nothing to lessen her obsession. The nonchalance with which Buddhism was practiced, the myths and superstitions stemming from the ancient Bon religion that antedated Buddhism in Tibet and had been attached to it, remained a constant source of irritation. Her Buddhist "awakening" had been, after all, in a museum. She was ill prepared for the reality as practiced every day among simple, unlettered Orientals. She had been imbued from childhood with the Protestant ideal of rigorous self-improvement. It was difficult for her mentality to accept the Oriental concept of a gradual unfolding of consciousness.

Sidkeong continued to be occupied with affairs of state. She missed their long discussions and the evening rituals. He presented her with a beautiful religious robe on the occasion of the New Year. Authorized to be worn only by high-ranking female lamas, the robe had been duly consecrated. This special gift filled her with delight, and temporarily lifted her spirits. But she had need of a project to occupy her time. She decided to learn Tibetan, which the Dalai Lama had urged her to master. A teacher was found who could come daily for instruction. But her physical discomforts continued to plague her.[3]

She decided to put an end to her boredom, and undertook a trip into the mountains to visit the area where, according to legend, Padmasambhava had lived.[4] There were four monasteries there, scattered in the forests. Along the way she encountered a group of merchants returning to Lhasa. "How impressive are these encounters with those who cross over the mountains, ascending higher and higher until they disappear, plodding on across the snow-covered steppes."[5]

She longed with all her heart to join them! But it was not yet the time for her to disappear among the mists.

During one of her monastery visits she was the guest of a very wealthy lama, who was also entertaining a colleague of her acquaintance, known to be an initiate of the highest tantric practices. During the night she heard him, in the adjoining room, preparing to celebrate his nocturnal ritual. Arising in the intense cold, she wrapped herself in her warm robe, and opened the door just a crack. The yogi was seated facing his disciple, his tambourine in one hand, a small bell in the other. On the carpet before him rested his singular trumpet, made

from a human tibia. Hour after hour the chanting re-
sounded in the crystal mountain air, accompanied by
the scanning of this eerie instrumentation. Alexandra
recognized it as a ritual normally celebrated not in a
private residence, but on a lonely isolated plateau where
the dead had been recently cremated. She was quite sure
her friend had performed it for her benefit and was
deeply grateful for this honor.

Like a gourmet, she savored the exotic treat of this
nocturnal concert. When it was finished, she closed her
door and slipped between the covers for three hours of
deep slumber.[6] No insomnia, no rheumatism, no intesti-
nal pains! Her body and spirit were in perfect accord, in
health and harmony.

A few days later as she moved along her route, she was
overtaken by Sidkeong. He was hastening to Gangtok,
having been alerted that his father was on the brink of
death. They paused for tea in a nearby bungalow. She
regarded him with solicitude, and wondered what he was
thinking—so close to his "throne of operetta in the State
of Offenbach." To Alexandra, Sidkeong seemed to be-
long to another world altogether. "I often have the
impression that he will mount a flying dragon or a
moonbeam and disappear among the clouds."[7]

At this particular time Alexandra was eager to find
public sources of financing for her projects, which would
ease the burden for Mouchy. She had requested a grant
from the French Office of Public Instruction to continue
her research in Hindu and Buddhist philosophy. When
she returned to Gangtok she received the disappointing
news that her request for funding had been turned down
by a certain Minister Viviani. He was a strenuous "anti-
clerical," opposed to any research of a religious or
spiritual nature. Alexandra was furious, believing that it
was just this type of response that would prepare the
ground for an equally unintelligent reaction in favor of
"sentimental religiosity." "There are few people capable
of being truly 'Free Thinkers,' who can do without gods

either to admire or insult; the insult is often an act of faith more profound than adoration."[8]

The trip to Bhutan she had hoped to make with Sidkeong was now called off altogether, triggering a bout of neurasthenia, but the happy result was a complete loss of appetite, and a few kilos lost, much to her relief. She hated being fat. In spite of her "awakened" state, she said how much it pained her to assume the shape of a "little round ball," she who had once been so gracefully slender.

News finally came of the maharajah's death, forcing Sidkeong to take up the political life he abhorred, and to face at last the fact of an imminent marriage. He had made it clear that he did not want to marry any of the princesses available for his selection. For a number of years he had had a mistress whom he adored, and with whom he had a son. He had frequently confessed to Alexandra how he could not bear the idea of an arranged marriage, and wanted his life to remain exactly as it was. This point of view was understandable. He had the best of both worlds, a lovely mistress and a "spiritual sister." A jealous wife could only complicate the situation. Nevertheless he was obliged to choose, and solicited Alexandra's advice in this delicate matter. With her assistance, he finally decided on a Burmese princess who was not only very pretty, but also intelligent and very modern in her viewpoint. This last quality filled him with terror, and it was the "spiritual sister" who did most of the corresponding with his future wife, explaining diplomatically that His Royal Highness was occupied with important affairs of state.

The circumstances of his accession were not easy. Former ministers of his father were very hostile to him, and would have preferred his younger (and more malleable) brother. To Sidkeong it seemed that the time of his life when he was free to be himself and to do as he pleased was irrevocably finished.

During this period Alexandra had an important

dream. She was in Brussels on the Grand Place, awaiting the passing of a procession. The place was decorated with flags, banners, and festoons of flowers, as for a festival. Crowds were massed everywhere, even at the windows. She became aware that she was dreaming, and that soon she would waken and all this would vanish. In the dream state she examined this idea with the realization that the same condition existed in her waking state, that everything appeared and passed in vivid sequence, moving away as though it had never been. The things observed and experienced in "real life" had no more authenticity than those in her dreams. This dream, so rich in symbolism, revealed, among other things, an important change in the role she was playing in Sikkim. Whereas she previously performed on center stage, alone, or in concert with Sidkeong, she had become primarily a witness. She had withdrawn from all participation. It marked a new stage in her development. The existence of a hermit seemed to her more and more appealing. The "call" of this isolated life of dedication, which seemed to open before her, became increasingly difficult to resist. She hoped to remove herself forever from that squirrel cage in which all those beings blinded by illusion turned and turned, animated by what she described as the "desire to exist" of Schopenhauer. The thought of returning to the mundanity of her previous existence filled her with horror. She hoped Mouchy would understand that this feeling did not emanate from a lack of affection for him. She loved him more profoundly than ever, and felt she understood him better than before. He was more truly loved, she told him, by his distant voyager than were his friends by their devoted spouses.[9]

The process by means of which Alexandra withdrew from the world was not without moments of pain and nostalgia. Philippe had taken a position in Bone, in Algeria, and had sold the beautiful home that they had shared. She loved her home, which she had decorated according to her taste, which contained her golden Buddha, her piano, her extensive library. She had always hoped to return to its spacious luxury for her final days, to settle down there at last and write the books that were germinating in her mind. Knowing that she could never return, that her home was gone forever, was a true test of her renunciation.

But in May of 1914 Mouchy had apparently presented her with an ultimatum. Reading between the lines she realized that another woman had replaced her, and he seemed indifferent as to whether she returned or not. She replied that there was absolutely no question of a legal separation or divorce. She carried his name with dignity and would continue to do so. She planned to return to him as a loving companion, but not as a sexual partner. Even the thought filled her with revulsion. She finished by commenting that since anyone else could fill her place, she was not obliged to fulfill a responsibility that could as easily be supplied by another.[10]

Alexandra's attitude reveals her as a woman with one foot in the nineteenth, the other in the twentieth century. She wanted to be accepted and appreciated for herself, for her mind and spirit, for what she had to offer as a person. She did not wish to be merely "possessed" as an object of pleasure. There are reasons for her lack of sexual response. Among these was the complete absence of any affectionate physical contact during her lonely childhood. But more than that were the implied attitudes of submission and possession inherent in male-female relationships of her time. For Alexandra these were unsurmountable blocks to any free expression of ardor. Only at a distance could she allow herself the luxury of expressing her very real feelings of affection for Mouchy. After reflecting that never had he wanted to share her mental life, she said, "For me that is what constitutes marriage, the true marriage. It matters little whether you sleep together or not. . . . The essential is the communion of spirit which is neither affected by distance nor the other contingencies of life. I know that you are far from sharing my views on this subject, but what can I do?"[11]

In her letters, often touching in their expressions of longing, she repeated how very much she would like to share the intellectual and spiritual discoveries she had made with someone, especially her husband. But she recalled that when they had been together and she tried to talk with him his only response was to distract her by caressing her legs and bringing her back to what was "really important." She had come to realize that in truth he only wanted someone to share his bed and that another could serve as well.

In Sidkeong, on the other hand, she had found an intelligent, well-educated man with whom she could share her spiritual life. She was probably never consciously aware of the depth of her feeling for him, or of the awakening sensuality that resulted from her contact with this romantic figure, though she often remarked that he seemed to have stepped from a fairy tale, a dream, or a myth. She always described their relationship as based on the models of mother and son or brother and sister, without considering that all human relationships are recapitulations of those early, most fundamental combinations. Although she was ten years his senior, her physical age would always be younger than her years, even when she was one hundred. Her courageous and persistent investigations often included self-examination, but this area of feeling was unexplored, potentially dangerous territory. Scaling the Himalayas was, for her, far less threatening. She could allow herself a certain emotional freedom because of the physical distance implied in the person of Sidkeong. She continually stressed his difference, his belonging to another world, another race, that she considered him a "personnage of opera." (It must be remembered that these remarks were being addressed to her husband.) Since his physical needs were well supplied by his mistress, Alexandra was safe. She risked nothing in falling in love. To what extent her feelings were returned is unclear. He obviously wanted to keep her near him. He repeatedly offered to build her a house of her own adjacent to the palace; or if she preferred, once he was respectably married, she could inhabit her own private apartments in the palace itself. Oriental princes could comfortably accommodate the presence of numerous women in their lives. Alexandra's projections upon this exotic and elaborate screen were fascinating. She identified with both the mistress and the future wife. She suffered with the mistress, whose child had suddenly died. Yet she hoped Sidkeong would eventually transfer his affections to the intelligent young Burmese princess (whom she had chosen for him). She neglected to take into consideration the workings of a karma that would in the end decide the issue.

The gomchen of Lachen had invited her to visit him in his summer retreat high in the mountains. Alexandra decided to accept, and began to prepare for her departure. She had adopted the British habit of travel, taking all her gear, her bedding, cooking utensils, and zinc bathtub with her, plus the servants and horses required to transport this mountain of equipment. She chose warm, flannel-lined *pantalons* (instead of multiple layers of skirts), several long coats, heavy riding trousers, three flannel shirts, and of course her religious robe and "bonnet." She had two presents for the lama, a thermos bottle that would provide him with hot tea in his hermitage, and a wristwatch with a radium dial. Before leaving, she cast one last remark in Mouchy's direction. If he refused to send her any more money she would simply remain in the Orient, living as an ascetic. She was convinced that she could face a life of poverty and renunciation in the Orient that would be unthinkable in France or North Africa. Being reduced to the level of "une petite bourgeoise" was too horrible even to contemplate. "I don't know that I could face a fifth floor on the courtyard at Grenelle or La Villette." This would be impossible because "inesthetique." Her capacity for indifference was as yet relative, but she hoped one day it might extend even to occupying a fifth-floor apartment.[12]

The availability of an apartment in the royal palace, however, was not included in this discussion of her capacity for indifference. Alexandra could if she chose, endure incredible privation and discomfort. But she could not support the idea of living in Europe without money, of "playing the role of a spectator." "The difference is great between the renunciation one has chosen and the impossibility of obtaining material things."[13]

She frankly admitted her aristocratic preferences and her taste for refinement. How many women of her time would have had the insight and candor to make the observations she did to her husband? "You are indeed an elegant monsieur. I remember that that quintessential aesthetic of those who are aristocratically raised caused me more than once to regard you from afar with pleasure, as a handsome object. I believe you are the only person in the world for whom I have a feeling of attachment, but I am not made for married life."[14]

There it was, concise, emphatic, and completely honest. She loved to contemplate his elegance—from afar. He could take it or leave it. He replied by sending a long letter with photos of "their" new home.

At this moment all other considerations were obliterated by an assassination in Sarajevo. War was unleashed on Europe. It would be some time, however, before the repercussions would be felt in the high mountains of Sikkim.

Before joining the gomchen, Alexandra decided to make an expedition into the high mountains of Tibet that lay just across the frontier near the lama's hermitage. She was accompanied part of the way by the maharajah, and by Silacara, a Scottish Buddhist who had come to live in the area. Although she found this man's brusque manners not to her liking, they arrived at a certain understanding, and he eventually translated her *Modern Buddhism* into English.

There were the usual gifts, flour, tea, and a length of yellow brocade from the prince, and the lively accompaniment of orchestral music as they departed, all in very high spirits. Moving along the caravan route that led into the steppes and beyond, she felt ancient memories mounting within her, "from the depths of centuries," and wondered if indeed she had lived a previous life as a nomad of Central Asia. The peaks and glaciers, the views of vast expanses punctuated here and there by ruined monasteries, were so exhilarating she could hardly describe them. She truly believed this to be her last great adventure.

Sidkeong was unable to go the entire route with her. As they reached the diversion leading to Choten Nyima, he turned in another direction. On this occasion he was wearing an Alpine costume. He disappeared, leaping from one boulder to another, turning from time to time to wave his hat, crying "Goodbye, don't stay away too long!"[15]

She would never forget.

The gomchen greeted her warmly and showed her to her "accommodations," a nearby cave where, with the help of her servants, she installed herself comfortably. One of the servants was a Tibetan boy of fourteen named Aphur Yongden, who early showed evidence of unusual intelligence and loyalty, and who would later play an important role in Alexandra's life. She began to concentrate on the Tibetan language and to teach the gomchen the rudiments of English. It had been his intention to embark on the traditional three-year, three-month, three-week retreat he undertook with great regularity, but he decided to concentrate instead on her instruction. As the snow began to fall, they descended to the monastery of Lachen. She installed herself in several rooms and prepared to endure the Himalayan winter.

The notice in her diary for December sixth is brief.

"Sidkeong Tulku died at three o'clock in the afternoon." He had mounted his flying dragon and disappeared among the clouds. It was a blow such as Alexandra had received only once before—on another cold December day in Brussels. It was rumored he had been poisoned, but how, or for what reasons remained lost among the political intrigues that had dominated his short life. A few days after this news arrived, Alexandra forced herself to witness the cremation of a woman who had died in the nearby village. Had she been in Gangtok she would have seen his small hand shriveling in the fire, like those of this cadaver. It was present before her as though she had been a witness. But she said to herself, "Et voilà, c'est fini . . . la vie continue."[16]

Subsequent reflection led Alexandra to feel that Sidkeong's sudden death had a certain poetic validity. She remembered how many times in recent months she had heard him exclaim, "Oh, how I would like to remain as I am!" His wish had been granted. His younger brother was installed in his place, and the Offenbach kingdom resumed its round of activities as though nothing had happened. The new maharajah and his young sister were also very devoted to Alexandra, and she was repeatedly invited to visit the palace. She always found an excuse to decline, finding it unbearable to see that place where she had spent so many happy hours.

The gomchen was devastated as well by the loss of this friend for whom he had the greatest admiration. He saw his disappearance as a death blow to their efforts at religious reform and teaching for the people of Sikkim. He was correct. Even the funeral ceremonies saw a return to practices Sidkeong had tried to suppress, and much alcohol was consumed during the ceremonies. The sharing of their mutual grief forged a bond between Alexandra and the gomchen that served to sustain them both during the ensuing months.

As a means of distraction she renewed her relations with the ladies of the Swedish Mission at Lachen, and

visited them from time to time. They had ceased their
efforts to convert her and she enjoyed the female company. One day the ladies made a visit to the apartment
she had arranged in the monastery. On the shelves she
had placed not only her many volumes, but certain
objects of religious and artistic significance, as well. As
the ladies were admiring them, one picked up a magnificent carved marble lingum Alexandra had brought back
from Benares. The young woman was entranced with the
object, caressing it with her fingers, and commenting on
the superb workmanship. She wanted to know exactly
what the image signified. At this very moment the
gomchen appeared at the open window and, regarding
the ladies, understood at once the direction the conversation had taken. Seeing the gomchen's sparkling eyes
and amused expression made it almost impossible for
Alexandra to keep her mien serious. She cleared her
throat and said, somewhat hesitantly, that the object
symbolized what only a married woman could possibly
understand. The poor woman flushed deeply and set the
lingum down as though it were a burning coal. "I thought
as much!" she exclaimed. Later the lama asked Alexandra to translate the exchange. He laughed and laughed.
"Will you write this to your husband?" he inquired.
"But most certainly," she replied, joining in his mirth.
For the first time since the death of Sidkeong they were
able to laugh. The dark spell had finally been broken.

Alexandra was moved by the gomchen's generosity. He
presented her with everything from butter to ancient
texts of museum quality. One present, which now resides
in a place of honor at Samten Dzong, in Digne, was a
rosary that had previously been in the possession of a
lama believed to have been a saint. It was composed of
one hundred rondelles, each carved from a different
human skull, with counters of silver and coral.

His human frailties both amused and comforted her.
He had secretly returned to his hermitage in search of a
kitten to which he was quite attached. He remained there

for several days, without food or bedding, hoping the little creature would return. The cat had in the meantime regained the monastery on her own, and when a messenger was sent to apprise him of this fact, he was furious to be discovered in his weakness for his small companion.

The relationship between guru and disciple was indeed complex, and many believed that it had to be worked out gradually between individuals who were spiritually attuned over many incarnations. The day the gomchen specified the terms of his contract with Alexandra, she wrote in her diary:

"I must promise to remain at his complete disposition for a year, at Lachen in winter, and near his cavern in the summer. . . . I felt my heart beat, and I had an instinct of withdrawal . . . and then I promised. Who wishes the end must accept the means."[17] Her apprenticeship lasted just short of two years.

During the winter the gomchen's life was far from that of a hermit. He had a sister who came from Tibet for an extended visit, and he also had a "companion." "This lama belonging to the sect Nga-Lu has not remained celibate. He is allowed to marry. He has not, but like many of his colleagues, he has a companion."[18]

She and Alexandra were congenial, and it was often comforting to have her sympathetic female presence in this predominantly masculine world. On one occasion she made Alexandra a gift of beautifully embroidered felt boots.

Early in the New Year there were the usual celebrations, eating, drinking Tibetan beer, dancing, singing, and sporting contests. Alexandra fled the noise and confusion with what looked to the gomchen like disapproval. He confronted this puritan attitude, saying her spirit was "sick" because she could not support the celebration of these childish, simple people. Her Huguenot inheritance often interfered with her appreciation of the philosophic nonchalance of Buddhist sages like the gomchen. She could not overcome her feeling of respon-

sibility to correct those who were "in error." The gomchen's attitude that human life was only a play of shadows on a cinema screen, that he himself existed only as a
shadow among others, she could accept intellectually,
but she was a long way from feeling it on a deeper level.
Her need to force on others the excessive standards she
set for herself was perhaps her greatest weakness. Her
devotion to the principles of Buddhism was unques-
tioned, however. As early as September 26, 1912, she
had entered in her diary that after Sidkeong and his
lamas had left the monastery she had remained alone
for some time, "and seeing no more the idols, but only
the great Dharma, I prostrated myself and swore that I
would follow the example of the master, and I wished no
other life than that of which my ascetic robe was the
symbol, consecrating myself to the mission conferred by
the Bhagavad to his disciples, which is to preach the
Dharma for the welfare of all beings."[19]

Life in the monastery of Lachen during the winter
months was punctuated with little dramas. One afternoon just as it was getting dark, Alexandra noticed a
small dog trying to make its way through the deep snow,
finally giving up, exhausted. Against the outcries of her
companions, she set out in waist-deep snow to rescue the
creature. She advanced slowly, beating a path with a
staff. One of her boys joined her, and a routine worthy
of Laurel and Hardy ensued. Each fell into a deep hole
and had to be rescued—they literally tumbled their way
to the dog, by now quite immobilized in the snow. She (it
turned out to be a female), half savage and very frightened, had little patience for their efforts to rescue her.
Finally they tied a rope around her and dragged her all
the way back to the monastery in complete darkness.
Alexandra adopted her and she became a most faithful
companion.

In April she had received a gift of money from the
maharajah of Nepal. With this donation she was instructed to build a small dwelling in which she could live

while continuing her studies. As the good weather advanced she became totally engrossed in the cabin she was planning to construct thanks to this generous gift. It would be located in front of the cave she had inhabited the previous fall. The construction was not an easy process with the very unskilled labor available. The first version tumbled down and had to be completely rebuilt. She called her "home" De-Chen Ashram, which meant "Great Peace." At last she could send for her many trunks left behind in Darjeeling and create a comfortable retreat. To her great relief, money finally arrived from Mouchy as well, having made its way across war-torn Europe.

The lama's cat moved in with her. Perhaps she preferred Alexandra's cuisine. The cat was very intelligent, and learned to pull the cord that rang the doorbell in order to be admitted. Another dog was soon added to the collection of animals that made up the "personnel" of De-Chen Ashram.

Mouchy referred to this abode as her "hôtel particulier." It consisted of one large room divided by a curtain into a work space where she wrote and studied, and a bedroom. The latter gave onto her cavern by means of a small staircase. A balcony included a bathroom, a corridor leading to the kitchen, and two tiny rooms, a guest room and storeroom for provisions. Another small building housed her domestics. The interior walls were covered with paper and the wood was painted. It was a rude shelter, but cozy, and she planned to stay there during the entire winter. For the New Year the maharajah's sister sent her a warm woolen carpet for the floor.[20] Undoubtedly the completion of her very own dwelling helped to ease the pain of knowing that her home in North Africa was gone forever.

She met daily with the gomchen for instruction, not only in the Tibetan language, but in tantric mysteries as well. They were frequently joined by erudite visitors from Tibet and India. Thus Alexandra profited from a wide range of teaching. It was not easy for her Western, democratic mentality to accept the attitude of these learned sages, whom she described as "transcendental skeptics," toward the ignorant masses under their tutelage. Their feeling was that these simple creatures could not possibly benefit from the esoteric teaching of Buddhism, and they allowed them to continue their pagan, animistic traditions. Only after many incarnations and virtuous lives would they possess the intellect needed to appreciate higher levels of understanding. Meanwhile the lamas felt it was a waste of time to point out the beauties of nature "to those who were blind from birth." The kindest approach was to help them to live as peacefully and happily as possible in their blind state. Philosophic concepts should be reserved for an enlightened elite. They could only destroy those with little or no intelligence. The concept of equality Alexandra had learned during the years of her European education did not accommodate itself to the intellectual armature on which the lamas' belief system was constructed.

News from the battlefields of Europe in 1915 was uniformly bad. Many pages of Alexandra's letters were devoted to commentary on the condition of war. She declared that although many had died, ideas—seemingly so fragile in the presence of such brutality—would survive a long time. They would survive men, natural catastrophes, and history; generations after generations would be nourished by them.[21]

She was deeply affected by the violence that was being played out on the battlefields of western Europe, and wondered what had been the fate of her mother in occupied Belgium. There had been no news of her for a long time. After many months of uncertainty, she learned that her mother had survived the German occupation and, though mentally incompetent, was still alive.

The gomchen was a man of contrasting moods—one day genial, the next day childish and provocative enough to make her weep with despair, or burst out laughing.

They would spend days and days reading and translating. Suddenly, in response to a question she might ask or a commentary that occurred to him, he would "light up like a lamp," inspiring her with an interpretation that would open wide the doors of understanding. It was, however, a slow process.

During the winter of 1915–1916 she had with her three young Tibetan boys and the mother of one, who saw to her needs. In her letters there begin to be occasional references to one of the boys, Yongden. He was of above average intelligence, of good family, and drawn to Alexandra because he wanted to advance his knowledge and experience. He not only had a lively sense of adventure, but a willingness to serve that was unusual in a young boy. Little by little he assumed more responsibility in the managing of the household. Frequently she retired into her cavern and saw no one for a period of time. Her meals would be placed in the adjoining room and a bell rung to inform her. Then, having finished her retreat, she would take the group, dogs included, on a little outing to provide some distraction. On one of these occasions the gomchen, his companion, and a little orphan he had taken in came to join them. After a rigorous game of football they built a big fire on the edge of the forest and made Tibetan tea. As they sat around the bonfire, the gomchen began to chant heroic legends of bygone centuries. She regarded the disparate group, remembering herself as a little girl engrossed in her volumes of Jules Verne. Her dreams had indeed been realized.

But one day a package arrived that caused a sudden onslaught of emotion. She had asked Mouchy to send her a favorite kimono. As she unfolded it she was suddenly transported to the salon of her former home, saw herself seated at her piano, and Mouchy, on his way to his office, coming to bid her farewell. She remained a long time holding the kimono close to her, fighting back the tears, aware that she did not possess the vanity to present

**Alexandrine David,
Alexandra's mother**

**Louis David,
Alexandra's father**

Alexandra, age three

Alexandra at eighteen,
in her presentation gown

**At the piano, Villa Hélène,
Tunisia, 1901**

**Philippe Néel,
Alexandra's husband**

**Alexandra in Tunis,
rue ABd'el Wahab, 1904–1911**

**Sidkeong Tulku,
Alexandra's "prince," 1912**

Sidkeong Tulku, 1912

Tibetan yogi dressed
for a ceremony

Tibetan yogi

Gomchen of Lachen,
Alexandra's teacher, 1913

Alexandra in lama's robes, Sikkim, 1913

Gyantze, May 1924

Bombay, 1924

Alexandra at the Catholic Mission
in Szechuan, May 1938

Alexandra and Yongden

Yongden, Alexandra's adopted son,
possibly in Italy, 1935

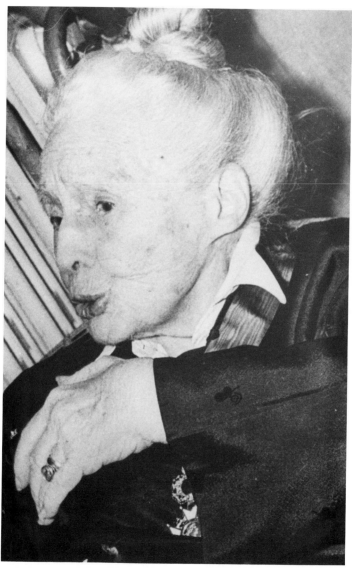

Alexandra as *commandeur* of the
Légion d'honneur, May 1964

Small buddha given to Alexandra
by Sidkeong Tulku

Samten Dzong, Alexandra's "fortress,"
site of the Fondation Alexandra
David-Néel, Digne, France

herself as stronger or more detached than she truly was.[22]

The deep snow arrived and made her meetings with the gomchen more and more difficult. When she arrived, covered from head to foot with snow, the lama's companion gave her a warm gown and slippers, taking her wet clothes to the fire and drying them for the return trip to her own cavern. The Tibetan New Year was celebrated in great style in the gomchen's cavern. All of them gathered together to regale themselves with a Chinese-style meal of multiple courses. This must have been provided by the gomchen's Tibetan companion, but how she managed to gather together the necessary ingredients remained a bit of her own "magic and mystery."

Except for an occasional attack of rheumatism, Alexandra's health during this winter was excellent. Even when she practiced the yogic exercise known as *tumo*, seated in the snow wrapped only in a thin cotton sheet, she never had the slightest sign of a cold. As a result of her practice of tumo, she was able to sleep with fewer and fewer covers during the night. She would not regret her initiation into this practice.

Although she had planned to remain in her ashram at least through another winter, the migratory instinct was beginning to manifest itself. She began to dream of the forbidden Tibet that lay so near—just across a barely defined border. She was quite aware of the possible reaction of the English governor if she ignored his very clear interdiction to cross this line. Nevertheless she made plans to do just that. She warned Mouchy that he must in no way mention the word "Tibet" because his letters were being opened by British censors. For this voyage she purchased a beautiful black mare that had a sad history. She had been bred to one of the Dalai Lama's finest stallions, but her colt had died. As a punishment, her owner refused her the corn he fed his other horses. Alexandra rescued her from this plight and saw to it that she received generous rations of corn.

As soon as summer arrived she set out with her caravan. "Don Quixote" had need of windmills to conquer.

On July sixteenth she and her party arrived in Shigatse. Alexandra's reputation had preceded her. The Tashi Lama and his mother were waiting to accord her the honors they felt were her due. In a letter she described her wanderings through the city of Shigatse, dressed in yellow silk, wearing the yellow "bonnet" of an abbess, a gift of the lama's mother. She ruminated how perhaps one of her ancestors had dressed like this. She would happily have stayed forever, which, in fact, they urged her to do. She was the guest of the lama's mother, indulging in delicious Chinese cuisine, wandering through formal gardens with European flowers, and meeting daily with learned lamas in the presence of the Tashi Lama. It was suggested that if she would remain, a house and servants would be provided for her.

The news of her escapade caused the English Resident of Sikkim, Sir Charles Bell, to lose his temper completely. He was used to being obeyed and this Parisian had indeed gone too far. Not only did she receive a notice to leave the country within fifteen days, but the people of Lachen were severely fined because they had not informed him of her intentions. The fact that the villagers had absolutely no knowledge of her activities mattered not at all to Sir Charles, but one day Alexandra would avenge their unjust punishment.

Perhaps it was what she needed to induce her to move on. Her lama preceptor was ready to begin his long delayed retreat. He had given her two years of his time. He had set her on the Path. It was now up to her to make of it what she would.

On September 2, 1916, she left her ashram forever. Immediately the furious natives of Lachen tore it down. But she realized that, like the fine sand one tries to hold in one's hands, the world is created of impermanence and perpetual change.[23]

Her descent to Calcutta involved spending a night in Darjeeling, in the same bungalow she had occupied in the spring of 1912, en route to her meeting with the Dalai Lama. A cycle had been completed.

9

The Miraculous Tree

«1916–1919»

The ship navigated slowly among small islands that emerged through veils of mist. For Alexandra it was pure enchantment, an unfolding of dream-like visions, one leading gradually into another, evoked by the gentle movement of the large vessel as it traversed Japan's inland sea. The dream metaphor had sustained her during the difficult period of readaptation to the "real world." All those months—her house built on the cliff, all that seemed never to have been. She might just as well have dreamed it.[1]

It is doubtful that even Alexandra David-Néel realized in 1916 the extent to which she had embarked on a legend of her own creation. She was simply moving on from day to day, unaware that she had plunged into a stream of history along with those whose exploits animate the mysterious darkness around campfires and hearthsides throughout the world. She herself had invoked the image of Don Quixote, and she wrote Mouchy of her eagerness to write an "Oriental Iliad." Yet who would have believed in 1916 that a woman, a small, rotund, middle-aged woman, would join ranks with Odysseus, Roland, Galahad, and Parsifal? She had followed the heroic path: she had responded to her own inner voice; she had completed the physical and intellectual trials; she had resisted the temptation to remain in a safe and comfortable harbor; she had experienced a romantic awakening, which had terminated in separation and death; she had retreated into the wilderness to strengthen her spiritual resources under the guidance of a sage, and had finally achieved the ritual of initiation, complete with all the mystically symbolic objects, the chalice, rosary, rings, mantles, and sacred texts. The most exacting mentor could hardly fault her preparation.

Finally, she had attracted Yongden, a devoted, loyal companion, who sustained her (often, quite literally, on his solid shoulders), and who, in the purest operatic tradition, served to provide the comic relief so essential to the survival of a legend. But the piece had its villains, namely time and lack of money. For although Alexandra had developed the ability to live outside the dimensions of time and space experienced by ordinary mortals, she could not escape the fact that it required five months for two thousand francs to travel from North Africa to Peking. This elemental fact would cause her discomfort, danger, neurasthenia, and colitis. It served to drag her constantly to earth, to block her passage, and constrain her movements. Amidst the war, pestilence, danger and inexpressible filth in which she moved, lack of money was the omnipresent menace.

When she had compared herself, leaving for Sikkim in the spring of 1912, to Don Quixote, she expressed the hope that her "windmills" would be of modest proportion. It was not that they were so enormous, these financial adversaries, but there were so many of them, and they were unending. There seemed never a moment of release from anxiety. Servants, bearers, and dignitaries stood always before her, their outstretched hands demanding the money already halved in value by exchange rates and wartime inflation. She would struggle valiantly against this situation, devise strategies to avoid it, employ hours of precious time entreating Mouchy to send larger sums, and more often, and then one day she would simply walk away from it.

Alexandra left Calcutta November 6, 1916, and finally

arrived in Kobe, Japan, February 7, 1917. Her reasons for visiting Japan were for the most part pragmatic. She was hoping to find a location in the Orient where Mouchy might be tempted to join her after the war. In the French colony in Tokyo, they could live beside the sea and he could indulge in his favorite sport of sailing. She also had the impression, which proved to be false, that life in Japan would not be too expensive. "I always professed that it is important to spend very little for what the vulgar call indispensable, and have plenty of money available for the superfluous."[2]

Finally, she wished to examine Zen Buddhism at close range. Her interest in the comparative aspects of religion was as strong as ever. She took with her only her tents and the minimum necessities in the way of personal effects. The Swedish missionaries purchased her beautiful black mare and her little donkey. One can assume that the gomchen saw to it that the cats and dogs were not abandoned, though they remained always with her, invisible companions, often referred to in her letters. And of course, there was Yongden.

During the two years he had served her, he had assumed a greater and greater importance in her household. In addition, he had chosen her as his religious mentor, and had indicated a willingness to accompany her wherever the next adventure would lead. When she was being threatened by her furious servants on the route from Shigatse, he had risen to dimensions of heroic grandeur. From keen observation of Alexandra during those two years he had learned something about the art of the theater. In most dramatic language, he told the servants to ignore the threats of the English governor, reminding them that the "whites" always stayed together, and that if she were harmed, the "natives" would be the ones to be instantly punished, and very severely. When at last they returned to Lachen he calmly took over, seeing to packing everything that was to accompany them, calming the excited servants, making his presence indispensable. His decision to leave Sikkim with her was not the nonchalant gesture that a young person of our time might make. He was the son of a solid, respectable family, with definite responsibilities. To abandon his family, his race, his culture, and leave with a white European woman was looked upon as desertion of the highest order. He would never be able to return. His inheritance would be forfeit. In Gangtok he took leave of her to go bid them farewell. To "make a good impression" she loaned him a handsome scarlet embroidered jacket. The family wept, pleaded, entreated, bargained, and threatened. It was of no avail. His return to Gangtok was accomplished in a torrential downpour. When, completely exhausted and soaked through to the skin, he finally reappeared, Alexandra was deeply moved. She had prepared herself never to see him again. But she said merely, "Go dry yourself. We'll have some hot tea." It was in this unusual circumstance that she, who had always congratulated herself on having avoided motherhood, was delivered of a son. From that moment they were absolutely inseparable, and the "story of Alexandra" became as well the "story of Yongden." She ultimately changed his name from Aphur to Albert and fitted him out in European clothes, which pleased him. Alexandra had separated herself from her parents, her lover, and her husband, definitively and without remorse. With Yongden she created a "couple" that would survive, untouched by the exigencies of life, the fury of his family, the jealousy of her husband. Death alone would separate them. She once commented to Mouchy that, had he been her son by birth, he would have been the one to go off seeking adventure, and she would have been obliged to sit home mending his socks and waiting anxiously for his return. But together they accomplished what neither of them could have done alone. They encouraged, sustained, inspired, and demanded the best the other had to give. At times they romped and giggled like two delighted children; at others they jointly immersed themselves in philosophic studies and esoteric investigations. Each was capable of making sacrifices for the benefit of the other, of nursing the other's illness and fatigue, of lightening with dry humor the many moments of discouragement along the way. Alexandra did not hesitate to take one of Yongden's slippers to him when he refused to leave his bed on cold mornings. But when he threw the slippers away and told her he'd had quite enough of that kind of coercion, she was intensely amused. He knew how to get around her. Those others, left by Alexandra as casually as dropped handkerchiefs, would have shaken their heads in disbelief.

Yongden was well equipped for his new position. He was extremely gifted in languages and could speak any number of dialects with ease, although he and Alexandra usually conversed in English. He possessed a strong young body and, in spite of an adolescent tendency toward laziness, he was always willing to give his best to any undertaking. He had inherited an oriental adeptness at bargaining that saved them on more than one occasion. Unburdened with Alexandra's baggage of occidental moral standards and false pride, he cheerfully teased and tricked his way through one near-disaster after another.

The steamship Cordillère took a long time from Hong Kong to Japan, and there were many stops along the way, among them Saigon. Returning after more than twenty years, she hastened to revisit her favorite zoological park, finding it in a sad state. "Where are the birds?" "Little birds all dead." "Where are the serpents?" "Little serpents all dead." She took Yongden and the other young Tibetan who had accompanied them this far to visit the large imposing cathedral, and attempted to explain the stories illustrated by the stained-glass windows. The young Tibetans were aghast. Used to the vivid descriptions of the magnificence of the palace in which the Buddha was born, they found it utterly dismaying that Jesus should have been born in a stable among animals.

It had been eight months since she had left Tibet, eight months of discomfort and adjustment. She compared the tango-dancing French diplomatic personnel on shipboard to a bunch of irritating nettles. She found their manners appalling and their conversations about big-game hunting filled her with disgust. She longed for her lost paradise of mountains, of solitude and peace.

But Alexandra approached Japan with a certain optimism. She had been in correspondence with a number of prominent Buddhists there for some time. Her numerous articles, as well as her book *The Buddhism of Buddha*,[3] had gained her renown in intellectual circles. In Japan she was treated as a celebrity and interviews were requested by numerous journalists. She was greeted warmly and installed at once in a lovely Zen monastery. Mrs. Suzuki, the wife of D. T. Suzuki,[4] made every effort to make her comfortable, to introduce her to important Japanese Buddhists, and to show her those places of greatest interest and beauty. But this was not the time for Alexandra to visit Japan. The humid, foggy weather depressed her. The food she found insupportable. She was plagued by physical discomforts and continuing nostalgia. In one moment of extreme longing she said to Mouchy that when at last she was on the point of death, she would wish that in her next life she might be reborn in a paradise composed of giant mountains and infinite steppes where, to the tinkling of yaks' bells, the "blessed" move in slow caravans toward the far horizons they would never reach. That was, for her, the greatest problem with Japan. There were no "far horizons." Her temple accommodations were picturesque in the extreme, but surrounded by enclosures of bamboo and evergreens. Tatami mats were no substitute for the rude canvas floor of her tent and the magic shadows created by her campfire.

Her reaction to Japan was not entirely negative. She

responded to the people, to their politeness, their grace, their eagerness to please. She loved the sounds that emanated from all the surrounding temples, the psalmodies, the solemn musical accompaniment to the sutras, the vibration of sonorous bells in the night. "All is quiet, peace, indifference, supreme detachment."[5]

But it was, on the whole, a place too civilized and occidental for her taste, too "tame," as the English expressed it. She was blocked there for some time waiting for money to arrive. When at last she received it, there was a piece of good news as well. Mouchy had accepted a new position directing the mines of l'Ouenza in North Africa. His income had increased to a point where she need no longer feel that he was depriving himself to send her the money she needed. Writing him from Kyoto in July 1917, she praised his professional and financial success, and believed that his good fortune was the result of all the sincere, positive wishes she had sent to him out of her deep appreciation. Yongden included a message as well. "Sir: I hear from my Lady that you are to do still greater things than before. My Lady looks very pleased and I beg you will kindly allow me to congratulate you. Your humble servant, Aphur Lama."[6]

The money Mouchy had sent meant she could at last escape from the humid climate of Japan, the overly-refined atmosphere, the monotony and "tameness." She left Kobe for Korea.

The crossing was not without adventure. Because of the extreme heat, Alexandra followed her custom of sleeping on deck in the fresh air. On the third night, however, a terrible storm arose. She slept in her soaked bedding, nonetheless, tossed by wind and waves as they approached the Korean coast.

But once again boredom and torpor set in. Everything now impressed her as banal, shabby, without interest. She repeated to Mouchy what she had said before, and would continue to express, that, having attained the summit of her dreams in the contemplation of those mountain heights, in the extraordinary vision of that snowy wilderness, there was nothing left to tempt her. She believed her life was finished, and there was nothing to which she might look forward with joy and longing. Although the air was cooler and more refreshing in the mountains of Korea, her stay was plagued by continual rainfall. She stayed in several monasteries, where she was welcomed with warmth and hospitality. Although she arose in early darkness to participate in their rituals and meditation, her inability to speak their language greatly hampered her communication with the monks. Alexandra never enjoyed playing the role of "tourist." She decided to continue her journey toward China. Pausing in Seoul long enough to have their passports renewed, they then departed by train for Peking, arriving October 8, 1917.

Throughout the misadventures of this dreary year, filled with so much disappointment, she continued to reiterate her appreciation to Mouchy, telling him that only the prospect of seeing him again would tempt her to return to Europe. In spite of the discomforts that had plagued her route since she had left Sikkim, she still preferred the Orient. And though she felt more "at home" in the presence of the English than the French, she preferred the oriental mentality to both, the oriental manners and way of seeing things. Above all, however, she was drawn to the empty vastness and solitude of the steppes and mountains.

"In all this, only you count. I want to see you, to thank you for all the happiness you have given me in allowing me to live for a few years the life of which I have dreamed since my childhood. You believe, my dearest, that you have done a great deal for me, but only I can measure the extent. It surpasses all you can possibly imagine."[7]

She was well aware when she made her forbidden entry into Tibet that Sikkim would be forever closed to her. She was willing to pay the price. Had Sidkeong not died it might have been different. She would have settled in as his "sister" and advisor, continued her research and efforts toward Buddhist reform, and waited for the English to change their attitude. But there was more to it. Alexandra had completed her years of apprenticeship and contemplation. It was time to move on, to follow the ways of the heart.

The months in Japan were not entirely fruitless. She encountered there Ekai Kawaguchi, who had been received by the Dalai Lama on the same day as she. He had managed to visit Lhasa disguised as a Tibetan monk, and eulogized on the marvels of his excursion. She carefully filed the information for future reference, and moved on to Peking.

Peking pleased her more than Tokyo. She found the Chinese more "sympathique" than the Japanese. With time, she had come to recognize the predator concealed behind the latter's mask of politeness.

She believed the little "Japs" to be the Boches of the Far East. The same spirit which inspired the refrain "Deutschland über alles" had penetrated Japan from the world of the court to the last street sweeper.[8]

She saw them as expansionistic, eager to "swallow" Manchuria, Korea, and China. Her comments in this regard were most prophetic, and she even predicted that the next great war would be between the United States and Japan. The Chinese, on the other hand, she found in a lamentable state of demoralization, like an elephant harassed by clouds of flies. Soldiers were everywhere, wearing ill-fitting European-style uniforms, presenting arms as the train passed, though the reason for this gesture was obscure. The impending civil war was evident everywhere she traveled.

In the drier climate, her health improved. She had a premonition that she must hurry to finish what she had to do, that she had little time left. It was true, she remarked, that her family was noted for longevity, but the desire to live "has been consumed chez moi."[9] She saw human existence as the continual effort of man to make life a torment. All those representations of "hell" as imagined by various religions struck her as childish and unrealistic in view of man's ability to make an inferno of this world.

Soon after her arrival in Peking she wrote Phillipe that it looked at present as though she would not be able to go on to Mongolia as she had hoped, because conditions were so unsettled. To remain in Peking meant living in the "world of Occidentals," of diplomats and missionaries, participating in a round of teas and official dinners. She had not come to the Orient for that. Her sole purpose was to complete, to the extent that it was now possible, her religious studies. She had no money to waste on expensive clothes and entertainment. She praised Yongden's devotion: "It is not very amusing to serve a woman of my age, as demanding as I am, and leading a life devoid of comfort; to be the same day, successively cook, launderer, secretary and tailor."[10] She requested Philippe to make sure, in the event of her death, that Yongden was reestablished in Sikkim with enough money to build a house. She emphasized that he was paid absolutely no wages, but worked solely for his clothes and nourishment, both of which were at times extremely meager.

For the moment she was unable to leave Peking, and winter was coming on. Because of the European war, returning to North Africa was out of the question. Women and children were not accepted on any passenger ships. She had found lodgings in the large Buddhist monastery of Peling-sse. Her apartment was filled with elegant but hopelessly uncomfortable ebony furnishings. It had been previously inhabited by an emperor before he ascended to the throne. She had been informed that all the important Tibetan scholars she had hoped to consult had left Peking because of a conflict raging along the Tibetan-Chinese border. There was really no one with whom she could continue her Tibetan studies. In a

letter written in mid-November she related her meeting
with Prince Koung, the minister of Tibetan and Mongolian Affairs. He had arranged for an interview for her
with a grand lama about to return to a region she had
always longed to visit, that part of Mongolia containing
the famous blue lake Koko Nor, and the monastery of
Kumbum. He graciously invited her to travel with his
party. He could not leave immediately, however, as he
was waiting for funds that had been promised him by the
Chinese. Meanwhile it had become extremely cold. Alexandra set up one of her tents in an enormous, unheated
room. Money was again running low and she and Yongden were reduced to eating one meal a day, doing their
own laundry, and having as heat only a small brazier.
Yongden continued to wear his thin cotton trousers. In
one letter written to Mouchy during this interminable
winter, Alexandra revealed the religious names chosen
by their sponsors at the time of initiation. She was known
as Yishe Ton-me, "Lamp of Wisdom," and Yongden was
Nindji Gyatso, "Ocean of Compassion." As it turned
out, the sponsors had chosen wisely.

In spite of the plunging temperature in her "Maison
Cathedrale," she managed to make use of her zinc tub
every day, and produced a number of articles in both
French and English. But there were many moments of
sadness and nostalgia. She thought of her father, of the
dreary life he had endured with her mother. She wondered what had become of the dogs she was forced to
abandon in Sikkim.

Then, wishing to rouse herself from these dark moods,
she often departed with Yongden to go sight-seeing, and
one time visited the famous Summer Palace.

The lama with whom she hoped to travel to Mongolia
was invited to visit the "Maison Cathedrale" to have tea
with "Lamp of Wisdom" and "Ocean of Compassion."
He arrived in splendor, wearing a long robe of red-gold
silk and a purple vest, preceded by three servants and
accompanied by two high-ranking associates. Alexandra

presented the few Tibetan objects she had brought with her for his inspection. To her delight the lama seized her tambourine and began to chant one of the ancient hymns she had heard repeatedly in Sikkim.

As the winter wore on, her money was running out and, worst of all, it became apparent that China was on the verge of civil war. On January 21, 1918, she received a letter forwarded by Professr D. T. Suzuki in Japan. It was to inform her that her mother had died in Brussels exactly one year before. Her inheritance was blocked in Belgium by the war, but she wrote Mouchy that if she predeceased him (an event she always anticipated), he was to inherit all of it, with the exception of her "debts"—two thousand francs to the gomchen and three thousand to Yongden.

Finally, on January twenty-fourth, they left by train. The begnning of the voyage was colorful and luxurious. Escorted to the station by at least fifty persons of importance, they were installed in a first-class compartment as guests of the lama. As they entered the province of Shensi, the civil war exploded all around them. They found themselves quartered in a miserable stable surrounded by a courtyard in which their horses and mules wandered at liberty, churning up a sea of mud and manure. One morning Yongden announced to Alexandra that there were three heads hanging across from their door.[11]

The war had indeed caught up with her. She never lost her sense of humor, however, and regaled Mouchy with accounts of visiting the WC with bullets flying overhead, as well as rising early to bathe in her zinc tub, just in case the rebels' siege should prevent her ablutions later in the day. Being deprived of her daily bath was to be avoided at all costs. A Protestant missionary sent wagons to carry Alexandra and her belongings to the relative safety of his mission. There, she waited out the siege of the city of Tungchow. In the midst of this carnage she took advantage of the "calm" resulting from a terrible cloudburst to rejoin the lama, who had preceded her to Sian-fou, the capital of Shensi. Here, they were checked once again, but under what Alexandra termed more "civilized" conditions. Life seemed to go on pretty much as usual, and she was invited to give lectures on Buddhism to the members of the city council, the governor, and assorted intellectuals. The University of Peking approached her about the possibility of publishing a Chinese translation of her book on Buddhism.

On more than one occasion, as they continued their tortuous route, Alexandra was called upon to treat wounded and ailing soldiers with her stock of medical supplies. She, who had once wanted to become a physician, was given many opportunities to practice medicine in war-torn China and Mongolia. She even lectured the populace on the dangers of syphilis, and the means by which it was contracted, but her audience refused to believe her.

On other occasions she was treated with great deference. A "tea party" was arranged in her honor, during which the assembled army officers recited the classics in an atmosphere that Alexandra described as "calm, indulgent skepticism." Soldiers bearing loaded revolvers in their holsters passed the tea, which was served in exquisite porcelain cups.

Pestilence, decapitated heads "decorating" the route, bullets whistling overhead, all this she had recorded with supreme detachment. But on May fifteenth, she gave in to a moment of sensuality. How marvelous and diverse was Asia! How delightful to be far from Europe, far from India, truly in China! The Asiatics seemed to Alexandra to remain in a world of beauty and grandeur, the door of which remained closed to the Occident. She simply overflowed with superlatives and enthusiasm.[12]

This fantastic journey continued, with frequent interruptions, across a land that had become impassable except with mules and rude carts. When she examined her body during her daily bath, she found herself to be black and blue from head to foot as a result of being constantly tossed from side to side in the wagon as they advanced over pitted and jagged roadbeds. On one occasion she was obliged to take the whip to her conductor, a man of giant proportions, who had become extremely insolent. This she accomplished with an expertise that sent him rolling in the dust, and caused him to become immediately more respectful in his behavior.

She was constantly searched out by those whose relatives were sick. She and Yongden would take off on a "medical tour," inspecting tongues, patting stomachs, and handing out such medication as might ameliorate the plight of these helpless victims of a war they could in no way understand. She never refused. It was her hope that a French doctor could be persuaded to demand that a supply of medicines from the Chinese government be sent to her. She knew that her reputation as a "doctor" would precede her to Kumbum, which was indeed the case. Her own health was excellent in spite of the rude conditions of her life and her meager diet.

She and the lama had parted company along the way, as she had decided to proceed directly to Kumbum without first accompanying him to his home as he had requested. So it was that July 12, 1918, after six months and almost two thousand miles of travel, she could exclaim to Mouchy: "Ouf! I've reached Kumbum!"[13] She went on to comment that the greatest difficulties of travel lay in the apprehension that preceded the departure. Once en route, everything was simple.[14]

Certainly this applied to Alexandra. She could support anything but inactivity. During those periods when circumstances forced her to remain in one place for a long period of time, her health was miserable. Once she had departed, whether on horseback, on foot, or bouncing along in a wagon, she experienced a "miraculous" recovery. She simply put one small foot before the other, unaware of restrictions of space or time. In June she wrote Mouchy that the year 1918 arrived without her

being aware of it. She and Yongden ate three cakes each,
by way of celebration, but on the wrong day. Often she
didn't know either the date or the day of the week. She
lived very comfortably without acknowledging this trivia.
As soon as she was installed in Kumbum, the horrors
and trials that had attended her crossing from Peking
were behind her and forgotten.

In *Magic and Mystery in Tibet*,[15] Alexandra devotes
an entire chapter to the monastery of Kumbum. In our
own time this famous monastery became well known
because of the fact that, appearing in a vision, it provided an important clue to the discovery of the fourteenth Dalai Lama, who was born in the near vicinity of
Dokham. After his recognition he was kept in seclusion
in this monastery in company of an older brother and
an uncle who were monks there, until the ransom required by the local Chinese governor had been paid.
Then, at the age of four, he was conducted to Lhasa.

In 1555, the Buddhist reformer and founder of the
Gelugpa, or "Yellow Hat" sect, Tsong Khapa, was born
in the place where now stands the enormous complex of
temples that constitutes Kumbum. The legend surrounding his birth recounted that a miraculous tree grew from
the exact spot where blood stained the earth at the
moment of his birth. Later there appeared on the leaves
of this tree various images, sacred markings, and the six
syllables "Aum Mani Padme Hum." The meaning of
Kumbum is "hundred thousand images." In Alexandra's
time this original tree was confined within a chorten, and
presumably was nothing more than a dry relic. In front
of the temple that enclosed the chorten had sprouted
another tree that was supposed to be an offshoot of the
miraculous tree and was venerated as such.

Because of its importance, the monastery had attracted many tulkus (reincarnated lamas) among its
residents. In discussing such subjects as tulkus, which
are open to a variety of interpretations, Alexandra ex-
haustively examines all points of view, leaving the reader

the freedom to draw those conclusions that seem appropriate. She is never didactic, and often reveals her own skeptical attitude, but makes no effort to force it on her readers. She clearly labels fact, legend, tradition, or myth as such.

Her home in Kumbum must have been a delight. Adjacent to one of the important temples, it consisted of a beautiful Chinese-style building surrounding a patio, which in turn gave onto the court of honor of the temple. The interior walls of the ground-floor apartment were covered with colorful frescoes representing Tsong Khapa and various Tibetan deities. Claiming that these vivid images would keep her from sleeping, she installed Yongden (whose sleep nothing could impede) in this apartment. She lived on the second floor, with a balcony overlooking the patio. The custom in this country was to sleep on a platform beneath which a fire could be lighted in cold weather. As a result, one froze on one side, while being roasted on the other. It was not only impractical, but dangerous, and on one occasion when they had answered a medical emergency and were forced to spend the night away from Kumbum, they narrowly escaped death from asphyxiation as a result of one of these poorly ventilated "ovens." The brilliant red and yellow decor of her apartment she covered with Japanese hangings to diminish the "garish" effect as much as possible. But what filled her with absolute delight was the complete silence that reigned over the monastery complex, in spite of a population of over thirty-eight hundred lamas. The population was heterogeneous. Some of the lamas were extremely wealthy and lived in a princely style, while others were very poor, and possessed only a single room. Poverty was not required of those who wished to follow the monastic tradition in Tibet. Moreover, the monks were allowed to engage in whatever commercial activity they wished, which was indeed necessary for many of them to survive.

Well before dawn the community was awakened by the

eerie sound of many conches being blown in unison from
the rooftops, a sound that might well be calling the dead
back to life. Immediately lights began to appear throughout the monastic city as the monks arose and moved with
haste, but in complete silence, toward the enormous
assembly hall. There, they all assumed the same motionless, cross-legged position, and began to chant the first
office of the day. This was accompanied by bells, trumpets, and drums. The walls of the hall were decorated
with frescoes and hanging scrolls depicting many buddhas and other traditional figures seated in meditation
in the flickering illumination of numberless butter
lamps. Behind these were dimly visible the gold and
silver reliquaries in which reposed the ashes or mummi-
fied bodies of previous grand lamas. At last the long
service was interrupted as bearers arrived with buckets
of steaming tea, flavored in the Tibetan manner with salt
and butter. Each lama produced, from beneath the folds
of his robe, a wooden cup into which the tea was poured.
To this welcome liquid one could add a portion of
tsampa, a roasted barley flour that was the staple of
their diet. This was breakfast. The same morning ritual
was repeated throughout this Buddhist region of Central
Asia every day of the year.

When they had left Japan for Korea the young Tibetan
servant had returned to Sikkim. Now the household was
once again enlarged to include a servant. A young Tibetan merchant from whom everything had been stolen,
he was in desperate need of money. He was quartered in
another part of the monastery, and came every day to
serve them. He was not only uncharacteristically immaculate, but talented and willing to do anything they
required of him. After he had departed at the end of the
day they would say to each other: "If he doesn't kill us,
he's a present from the gods!" It was only partly in jest.
In that part of the world murder was considered a
banality. Everyone kept a rifle or pistol beside his bed
at night.

On October fifth she received word from the bank in Peking that the money Mouchy had sent in May had at last arrived. She wrote him a detailed account of her daily schedule. When the morning conches sounded at five o'clock, she had been awake for some time. Beneath a sky still alive with brilliant stars, she took a turn on her balcony. Yongden then arrived to build up her fire, and shortly after, the "gift of the gods" brought her morning tea. She then occupied herself with her toilette, some reading, and another promenade in the fresh air while the domestic cleaned her room. At nine o'clock she was served a complete English breakfast, the most important meal of the day. This was followed by study and translation with a noon break for the all-important ritual of the daily bath. At four o'clock she ate a supper consisting of soup and cooked dried fruit. Then more translation and study until nine o'clock, at which time everyone in the community went to bed. There were included in this regime many hours of meditation as well.

But occasionally she allowed herself a day of distraction. On one of these, after she and Yongden had paid a medical visit to a patient scratched by a playful monkey, they decided to go for a brief "climb." This quickly developed into a major excursion, as they teased each other to mount higher and higher. When they finally returned to Kumbum late at night, the gates had been closed. The sleepy guards, alerted by their cries, were astonished to discover they were still outside the walls. On another day they climbed for five hours, traversing six high passes, to visit a hermitage lost among the silent peaks. It was situated in a small grove of golden poplars on an outcropping shelf of rock, and once again her longing for De-Chen Ashram was awakened. She was reminded of her abandoned animals as well, when a large mastiff joined the monastery to which she was attached, and paid her a daily visit.

The winter brought with it an epidemic of Spanish influenza that killed over one thousand people in south-

ern Kansu alone. Both Alexandra and Yongden caught
the disease and were extremely ill with high fevers for a
long time. Their recovery took many weeks.

She was greatly cheered on the twenty-first of December, however, by news that the war in Europe was at last
finished. Peace had been achieved in Europe, but in
China war had arrived on the frontier of their province.
The route to Peking had been blocked, and many for-
eigners massacred. If the situation became really dangerous she planned to travel six days to the north to visit a
lama friend who lived at the other end of Lake Koko
Nor.

In October of 1918 Alexandra turned fifty. She was
still experiencing regular menstruation without any discomfort, and could withstand long hours on horseback
or many miles of hiking without tiring. She attributed
her excellent health to the rudeness of her life and her
simple diet. But the truth of the matter was that she was
at last leading the life she most loved, a balance of
activity and contemplation, of long days spent in studying the scriptures that abounded at Kumbum, and of
frequent excursions among the high mountain passes.
On several occasions she made fairly extensive explora-
tions into the neighboring areas to visit other monasteries and hermitages, as well as the famous "blue lake" of
Koko Nor. But the major part of her "voyaging" was
interior. Her morning meditation began at three o'clock,
after which she lingered on her balcony in the freezing
air until the crystal stillness was shattered by the into-
nation of hundreds of conches. The literary resources of
Kumbum were limitless, and she had become adept at
translation. Among other works she had attacked with
vigor was the Tibetan version of the *Prajña Paramita
Sutra*, which she was translating into French.

One January afternoon an important personage, the
lama "incarnation" of her temple, paid her a visit. They
sat huddled beside her stove talking of many things.
Suddenly a confusion of memories, impossible to control,

arose within her mind, memories of similar experiences, of similar garnet robes, of similar conversations, impressions of other times and other places. The need she had experienced to return to such a place as Kumbum had been so precise, so insistent, and accomplished under virtually impossible conditions in spite of war, disease, and enormous distances. Once there she had experienced the same rejuvenation she had known at Lachen during her retreat, the same spiritual calm, the profound knowledge that she had indeed arrived in a place where she belonged. The other indication that she had followed the call of a previous incarnation was the way in which she had been "recognized" wherever she went throughout the Orient. The most erudite sages had responded to her, even in places such as India, where Buddhism was looked upon with aversion, as one who merited respect and veneration. Lettered men not only listened to her with interest, they continually requested her to tell them even more. She was that most disdained of persons, a white European, and a female, yet even the simple, unlettered people she encountered recognized her spiritual power and bowed before her, asking for her benediction. She herself never took this very seriously. As she fulfilled their requests, she inwardly smiled the skeptical smile of the rational Parisian, and yet . . . and yet, the "memories" persisted.

10

The Eye of the Storm

«1919–1921»

The lake lay before them, an enormous turquoise set among grass-covered hills. The horizon was unbroken. Not a dwelling, neither a human form nor the shape of a grazing beast could be seen. After days of wandering across an uncharted wilderness, Alexandra and her party had reached the shores of Koko Nor.

She had used, as an excuse for this excursion, the nearness to Kumbum of increasing military activity—Chinese against Chinese, and Chinese against Tibetans—and had accepted the invitation of a lama who lived on the shores of Koko Nor to pay him an extended visit. But, in truth, it was because Alexandra could never remain sedentary for long, even among the literary treasures of Kumbum.

She had devoted the winter to copying a number of Tibetan translations of philosophic tracts, and had remained in strict seclusion. The Sanskrit originals of the works had disappeared, and her ambition was to make both French and English translations of these rare documents.[1] She reappeared from her retreat on the occasion of the anniversary of the death of Tsong Khapa, founder of the Gelugpa sext, to participate in the colorful activities, and to hear Yongden take his turn at blowing the conch, which he accomplished with great skill. The curtains were then rehung on her balcony to indicate that she was not to be disturbed. But preparations were begun for a departure. Mules were purchased, and Yongden set about organizing a caravan. In May she commented to Mouchy that the most effective "Fountain of Youth" was a life that combined travel and intellectual activity. Alexandra was becoming restless.

They set forth early in July. Along the way there was much arguing and discussion about the most direct route. A misunderstanding created by conflicting accents caused them to miss an important turn and become hopelessly lost. Finally, in exasperation, Alexandra marched ahead, snapped the Tibetan equivalent of "shut up!" and commanded them to follow her in silence, as she allowed her well-honed instincts to lead them back to the correct route.

The following night a group of horses, excited by the radiance of a full moon, broke tether and escaped. When, after hours of chase, they were corralled and soundly thrashed as punishment, Alexandra was convinced that her dearly loved "great mule,"[2], which had formed an amorous attachment to one of the horses, actually shed tears of sympathy. Alexandra was always moved by the suffering of animals.

The "promenade" was not without excitement. The possibility of attack by brigands or isolated bands of soldiers was omnipresent. Any unidentified silhouette on the horizon posed an immediate threat. In addition to Yongden and her servant, Alexandra was accompanied by numerous servants and a military escort. Everyone, including Alexandra herself, was well armed and on the ready, especially at night.

Their unfortunate delay had caused her lama-host to assume she was not coming, and he had already departed for the summer pastures with his numerous herds and flocks. It may have been a safety measure as well. The Dalai Lama had issued a proclamation to all the monasteries of the regions of Koko Nor and Amdo (long under Chinese domination) that this was the moment to strike for independence.[3] The vulnerability of China, now torn by civil war, gave the Tibetans an enormous advantage.

But military operations always put herds and flocks of animals in danger of being requisitioned or simply "borrowed." This lama, an erudite intellectual, was nonetheless a great herdsman. Alexandra compared him to the Old Testament patriarchs. He possessed three hundred horses, thousands of sheep, and as many beasts of burden, such as yaks. He was one of those who combined his mystery and magic with commercial shrewdness.

Yongden went in search of their host, returning with a pressing invitation to join the lama in his summer pastures. Alexandra had dreamed of summering beside the turquoise lake in the lama's house, but it seemed wiser to follow him. Koko Nor was situated at an altitude of about ten thousand feet. During the dry summer season there was little pasture for her pack animals, and the party was in constant danger of being attacked by thieves. But even the presence of danger could not dull Alexandra's appreciation for the colorful aspect of adventure. One evening they had three interesting visitors. They were presumably members of the indigenous Bon sect and had lived the nomadic life of the plains for many years. Their long leather overcoats, once lavender, had faded to a soft rose-blue shade under the assault of many seasons of rain and wind. Visible beneath were touches of brilliant orange garmets, and their right arms, left free according to local custom, revealed the sleeves of crimson jackets. Weather and dirt had rendered their faces a dark, nutlike color. As they stood there in the evening light against a background of pearly-opal lake, Alexandra reflected that it was a feast for the eyes, a joy to watch the movement of those colors, at the same time so warm and gentle. Unforgettable![4]

She eventually rejoined the lama among his flocks in a swampy, wet region with little scenic interest. Although the lake itself was magnificent, the surrounding marshy steppes were to her completely uninspiring. Her host, on becoming aware of her disfavor, found her quite lacking in taste, but allowed her to establish herself and her retainers at a little distance on a higher and drier elevation. Obsessed by the welfare of his beasts, the lama had no interest in the religious and philosophical discussions to which she had looked forward. Nevertheless she remained for several months, and found that the extended period of living out of doors benefited her health and caused her to "saunter like a rabbit."[5] But she was eager to return to her elegant apartment at Kumbum, to the daily round of rituals, and her beloved manuscripts.

By mid-November she was again settled in among these delights. The daily routine of meditation, translation, and mild exercise had been reestablished. As she and Yongden strolled through the monastic city, they could hear the chanting of distant celebrations, accompanied by an eerie combination of kettledrums, cymbals, and oboes. At the same time that she found all this enthralling, she viewed the lamaic institution itself with a certain skepticism. She compared the lamas' simplicity of mind with their European counterparts during the Middle Ages. Many of them were completely ignorant of the meaning of the texts they venerated. But all their primitive faults disappeared, reducing all ugliness, dirt, and rudeness to the level of a calm half-smile, that of the Buddhas who had understood the secret of the mirage and are disturbed by nothing.[6]

She set to work copying a collection of the works of Nagarjuna, the great Buddhist philosopher of the Mahayana tradition, wishing only that she were twenty years younger, there was so much she wanted to accomplish. In January of 1920 she also began the translation of the most interesting pages of the *Prajña Paramita Sutra*, with the object of including them in a book on the philosophy of Tibetan Buddhism. Day after day, wrapped in heavy robes against the intense cold, she pored over the manuscripts. Her efforts were tireless, for it was an occupation that filled her with delight.

Her letters to Mouchy during this period are filled with interesting requests. In one she asks him to send six pairs of heavy wool stockings, six pairs of heavy, brown cotton stockings, a long, heavy vest knitted, if possible, of dark red wool, a book of practical medicine, books of anatomy and gymnastics, and, finally, interesting post-cards of North Africa to send to the Tashi Lama's mother. In another she requests her necklaces of coral, amber, and other semiprecious stones that could be used as barter if necessary on her proposed trip. In still another letter she described in detail an aluminum fold-ing camp-bed she would like to have constructed for her. She sent to a mail-order house in Chicago for heavy boots, at the then exorbitant price of $5.75. Also in-cluded in these long epistles are pages and pages of advice to Mouchy on his health, his diet, his travels, business, expenses, investments, and all the minutiae of daily life. She reiterates again and again that if she suddenly disappears he should not try to find her. She will be trying to conceal her traces. If she were to die on the way, he would eventually be notified.

It became increasingly clear to her that there was only one possible route of escape—through Tibet into India. In 1920 she was surrounded on three sides by war: Sino-Japanese, Chinese-Tibetan, and the Bolsheviks in Mon-golia. Typhus and influenza were raging throughout the area. Much as she loved her life in Kumbum, it was proving to be too expensive. As a woman she could not become a permanent member of the community. She decided that when she had completed her translation of the twenty-one volume *Prajña Paramita Sutra*, she would move on. She had great hopes of returning to North Africa by way of the United States, where she would have been welcomed as a lecturer. She was eager to begin earning money with which to repay Mouchy. She made a formal will, leaving everything belonging to her in Asia, plus three thousand francs, to Yongden. Mouchy would inherit the remainder of her estate. Hours of consideration were devoted to how they might arrange their lives in the event she did survive to return to him.

One possibility would be to purchase land in the country and construct two separate houses, one for each of them, with a large garden to supply them with food.

Lack of money was becoming a major concern once again. Devaluation in both Europe and Asia had seriously diminished her resources. She could not leave Kumbum until she had paid her numerous debts. They began to sell everything of value they possessed, Yongden proving to be wonderfully skilled in this regard. She authorized Mouchy to borrow against her inheritance in Belgium. With this money she could pay her debts and move on. But "moving on" implied an eventual return to European life, a prospect that filled her with anxiety. And where would Mouchy decide to spend his retirement years?

Although Alexandra spoke of herself always as a "Parisienne," she had little affection for France. She spoke in open derision of the French mentality, and France was the one country where she could not imagine living after her return. (The Italian Lake District was as close to France as she would consider settling.) The thought of living the life of a "petite bourgeoise" was so repugnant, she was wont to say she preferred death by starvation in a Mongolian cave. Alexandra's socialist sympathies never extended to allow the possibility of leading a proletarian life without servants and necessary comforts. Again and again she repeated this theme, never apologizing for her aristocratic tastes. To scrub floors and change beds in a hospital to aid the suffering was quite allowable, even commendable, but to do it for oneself—never! She was used to traveling always as an aristocrat, paving the way with generous gifts and tips, according to the prevailing custom. She could face war, pestilence, and the rigors of inclement weather with equanimity. She could remain eight hours in the saddle and face brigands, armed only with a revolver. But mediocrity was beyond her.

Nine years had passed since she had seen Mouchy. Yet it would seem that this long absence had increased her esteem and affection for him. In September of 1920 she evoked the solitude of Central Asia, where she often thought of Mouchy as she lay in her small tent beside the bivouac fire of evening, in the silence of the immense desert. She told him that if she died—and if they followed the local custom that was dear to her, leaving her body on some height where the vultures could feed upon it—her last thought would have been a wish for his happiness and a feeling of deep and sincere gratitude for his devotion.[7]

She who once had declared that she was capable only of a "great love" had perhaps found it where she would have least expected it to exist. But Alexandra was possessed by an even greater love. In response to Mouchy's entreaties to return, she could only reply that to have returned at this time would have been to tear herself away from life itself.[8]

One morning, standing in the great courtyard beside her small house, she noticed a large group of camels being loaded for departure with a caravan that was destined for outer Mongolia. Above the mountains that surrounded the monastic city, the miraculous blue sky stretched in cloudless splendor. The deep silence was broken only by the distant sound of gongs and trumpets. Suddenly she realized the extent to which she was captive to these sounds and sights, to this nomadic calling. Were they teasing her, out of some previous incarnation, saying, "Follow, this is your ultimate destiny"? Wars and pestilence, the lack of resources that stood in the way, were as nothing before the force of those mysterious demands. In July she wrote that if she could bring herself to leave Asia it would be with the hope of ultimately returning to finish her days among the steppes, with a great space stretching before her and the blue sky over her head.[9]

Her calculations indicated that the proposed voyage would cover at least six thousand miles. To Mouchy she sent detailed instructions. He could write to her after one year at the Catholic Mission of Sinin, where she would leave all her baggage and books. He should not on any pretext try to locate her. No news would mean that she was in good health and all was well. He should speak of her project to no one. The success of her venture depended entirely on her not being recognized by the authorities.

The news from "outside" became worse and worse. Six provinces of China were suffering from famine and the resulting pillage and violence. In Chengtu five hundred people were dying each day of cholera. In Sinin it was typhus that raged. The Russians had descended on Mongolia.

Yongden had reached an important decision. He had postponed his final consecration as a Buddhist monk because he had held open the possibility of returning home to a lay existence and marriage. After much consideration during their long stay at Kumbum he had decided to finalize the rites of his vocation. This he wanted to accomplish before their departure. He still hoped always to remain with his adopted mother, and return with her to Algeria. She outlined to Mouchy all the reasons why she would not wish to separate herself from the companion who had shared so many adventures with her. When Yongden had left Sikkim he had renounced all claim to his inheritance. She felt that she owed him some future security. But the truth (and she freely acknowledged it) was that she had become completely dependent on Yongden. She could not imagine life without him.

The prima donna within had not been effaced by the years of religious searching. She responded with derision to news from Europe that "our immortal Sarah [Bernhardt]," though marching toward her eightieth year on a wooden leg, continued to grace center stage, and that Isadora Duncan still attempted to lift her one hundred eighty pounds in imitation of the sylphs. Yet Alexandra's self-imposed "retirement" was approaching an end, and she began to rehearse her own spectacular production. In spite of continuing danger, she and Yongden began to make extended excursions into the area. She wanted to be in top form when they left. One outing included the search for a rumored Taoist temple frequented by a famous hermit. It was situated at the summit of a steep incline, leading between sharp cliffs. As was her custom, Alexandra went off on her own and became separated from the rest of the party. The faithful Yongden finally retrieved her. Not in the least anxious, she was seated in all tranquillity, munching the luscious wild strawberries that had tempted her off course.

The last of the three years she spent at Kumbum was a time of searching and ultimate decision for Alexandra. She had been absent for ten years—years which for her had been fleeting, but which for Mouchy had dragged in boredom and loneliness. Difficult and eccentric as she was, Mouchy missed his unusual consort. The always available replacements did not satisfy his need. He continued his entreaties for her to return as soon as possible. They were not ignored, and produced much soul-searching on her part. Yes, she would return—but only when she had completed what she had set out to accomplish. What exactly that was remained a mystery, even to Alexandra. But she was possessed by a secret and insistent itinerary that would not be ignored.

The omens were anything but propitious. Bad weather had caused the potato crop to rot. There would be famine in the area as a result, and pestilence would continue to rage. The New Year of 1921 was ushered in by a devastating earthquake. Kumbum survived, but many villages were completely swallowed up and thousands of people perished. The Christian missionaries announced the imminent reappearance of Christ to judge the world. But disasters, natural or otherwise, were never adequate to deter Alexandra and Yongden. On February 5, 1921, they left Kumbum. It was a sunny day—one of those days when the blue sky shone in splendor above the yellow earth of China.[10]

11

Where the Sky Is Blue
«1921~1923»

The caravan had attained the last summit from which Kumbum could be seen. Alexandra and Yongden knelt in the deep spring snow to place several sticks of lighted incense among the rocks in honor of Tsong Khapa, the founder of Kumbum. Through the blue veil of drifting smoke the gilded roofs of the sacred city reflected the brilliance of the sun, now high in the sky. One could still identify the red and white temples and other buildings that composed the enclave. As they bowed silently, Alexandra was filled with deep emotion. She could happily have spent the remainder of her days there, on the threshold of the vast empty solitudes of Central Asia, exploring the sacred texts in the great library. But as a woman she was prevented from becoming a permanent member of the community, and her inveterate sense of timing had indicated it was time to move on. She had vowed to visit Lhasa, the city the English had forbidden her to see. It represented the last stop on her invisible itinerary of return to the West, and it was toward this end that she finally set out on February 5, 1921. Her projected route should have required a maximum of three months. Instead, three years of wandering in slow circles through western China, southern Mongolia, and eastern Tibet would pass before she achieved her goal.

The most direct way would have been to retrace her steps toward Koko Nor and join the main caravan route to Lhasa. But she was well known in this region, and she was convinced that only by maintaining the strictest incognito would she be able to enter Tibet. Her skin was already darkened by the sun. Dressed in her religious robes and bonnet, accompanied by an authentic lama-tulku son,[1] she easily gave the appearance of a dame-lama on a pilgrimage. She set out in the direction of Lanchow, from where she planned to descend along the Sino-Tibetan frontier between the regions of Kham and Szechuan. Not only did this entail a more rigorous route over high mountain passes and through deep river valleys during the worst season of the year, when they were inundated by spring floods, but there was the risk of encountering the rebellion and vandalism that accompanied the continuing military activity in this hotly contested region. It would seem that Alexandra was not in a hurry to reach Lhasa. She knew that, at least psychologically, it represented the last stop of her great adventure. Once that exploit had been achieved there would be difficult decisions to make, plans to execute, a meeting with a husband she had not seen for over ten years. About this uncertain future she could write pages and pages while she was as yet far away from it, but the reality could not be forever postponed. Inexorably these future speculations would have to be dealt with in the context of present experience. Meanwhile she possessed excellent health, a devoted companion, four loyal servants, seven mules, one horse, and enough money to last for some time. From the balcony of her little house in Kumbum she had watched caravans departing for the vast steppes and limitless plains of that land which lay beyond the farthest horizon. Her heart had followed longingly after each departure. Now it was her turn. The life of nomadic wandering that had beckoned insistently was within her reach at last. It is remarkable when one considers that this elegant, fastidious woman, who had performed first before the king and queen of a European court, then on the operatic stage in all the major dra-

matic roles, found her last and greatest fulfillment
astride a "great black mule" as she traversed the emptiness of Central Asia. The days of performing were behind her. No longer did she lecture before gatherings of
lamas, nor expound the doctrine seated on a throne. Her
only audience consisted of a handful of servants and the
(often skeptical) Yongden. The long search had finally
ended in a remote and deserted land where activity was
reduced to putting one foot before the other along a
tortuous route that seemed to lead nowhere. Her foot-
prints in the dust were as quickly effaced as her words
that evaporated on the wind. Her one desire was to
become invisible, to leave behind all recognition and
acclaim, to be simply an anonymous pilgrim in the
trackless wasteland. Even the goal of reaching Lhasa
receded before her. It would almost seem that she had
an unconscious desire to postpone indefinitely this "final" destination. Destinations had ceased to be important. Only the journey mattered, and no difficult conditions of weather or the route could diminish her joy. She
had truly entered on the Way. Traversing the wilderness
would assume the reality of metaphor as she pursued
her inner journey.

The beginning was punctuated by a bit of unexpected
comedy. During the years she had remained in Kumbum
she had availed herself of the services of an English
Protestant missionary at Sinin who cashed her checks
on the account she maintained at the bank in Lanchow.
This bank had notified her that "the reverend" had
transferred all her money into his own account. (It is
difficult to understand how it had been possible for him
to do this, but it had been accomplished.) When she
arrived in Sinin and asked him to give her the money in
question, he responded evasively that he had sent it to
her by nonregistered mail at Kumbum. Since she had
never received it, he commented only that he was very
sorry, but her money "seemed to be lost." After numerous telegrams from Alexandra to his superiors, the

money was suddenly "discovered" and she was reimbursed. While she was worrying about the possibility of being attacked by robbers en route, a clergyman had almost succeeded in making off with her funds before she had even set forth.

The land through which they traveled contained very few inns. Accommodations had to be requested in private dwellings, not only for the six travelers, but for their travel-worn beasts. Yongden often occupied himself with this important task. He would select a likely house or farm, knock vigorously, and request shelter for the night for the *khadoma* of Koko Nor and her party.

Khadomas were considered a special kind of feminine spirit that reincarnated from time to time. For the simpleminded and the superstitious it was easy to imagine that Alexandra was indeed such a creature. But during her long stay at Kumbum a number of very erudite lamas had confirmed that she did indeed deserve this status. She responded to such "elevation" with her customary humor and pragmatism. It was in no way disagreeable to be so considered. The advantages were obvious for a small, middle-aged woman traveling through dangerous territory with a minimal escort. Besides, she was of the opinion that, if there were no way of proving that she was a khadoma, there was no way of disproving it either. To attempt to do so would, in fact, be insulting to those who had elected her to such rank, and an outright act of ingratitude. She remained therefore "Khadoma," and with practice she began to believe that in fact she was, perhaps a little.[2]

It would seem that her acceptance of this state brought with it a certain good luck. When on one occasion she was obstinately refused entrance by an elderly Chinese gentleman, they succeeded in finding lodgings with a Moslem family nearby. The next day they discovered that, had they spent the night in the other house, she would have slept on the very platform where a leper had

spent many months and had died only four nights previously.

The beginning of her voyage was saddened by the
illness and ultimate death of the two puppies she had
decided to take with her from Kumbum. She suspected
them of having rabies. Because she was a dame-lama,
surrounded by devout Buddhists, it was out of the question to put them out of their misery. She tenderly nursed
the small creatures through their agony, holding them,
caressing them, talking gently to them, oblivious to the
danger to herself. It must have evoked for her the specter
of previous loss and separation, for she digressed at
length on the subject of her sorrow.[3] Animals had the
power to awaken in Alexandra the maternal gentleness
she normally took great pains to conceal. She was constantly concerned about the saddle sores suffered by her
pack mules, and would remain for days lodged in filthy
rooms or under rain-soaked tents waiting for them to
heal before continuing the route. Whenever possible she
hired additional beasts to lighten the burden.

She also showed a deep concern for the feelings of her
bearers and servants, even going so far as to override
her own values. Once they came face to face with a long
caravan of over a hundred camels in a narrow lane that
led between high walls, making it impossible to turn
around. Her own instinct was to back out with her
relatively small equipage, and allow the others to pass.
But she was well aware that to her men that would
amount to a terrible loss of face. Consequently, they
might not give her the respect and trust that might well
be crucial on this dangerous journey. That they have
confidence in her as a leader was of absolute importance.
Therefore she held firm, and the camel drivers were
forced to reverse their beasts, a long, difficult procedure, accompanied by multiple threats and oaths. As
she passed by them, her head held high in true oriental
fashion, she let fall a substantial sum of money in such a

way that her own retainers would not notice. Thus, everyone was satisfied.

In regions where bandits were a danger, she always walked well in advance of the others, pretending to be a solitary old woman, of no interest to robbers. In this way she served as the "look-out" for the caravan.

In one circumstance when they came unexpectedly on a group of obvious thieves, she quietly asked the nearest of her retainers to withdraw an automatic pistol from its place in her saddlebag, "just in case." The frightened young man was so distracted he grabbed her thermos bottle instead of the weapon. Laughing heartily, Alexandra sat down, poured herself a cup of hot tea, and invited the intruders to join her. They laughed in turn, and moved on. Whenever danger threatened thereafter, her response was "Perhaps it is time for a cup of tea!"

Her role as khadoma could on occasion be very fatiguing, when she was required to receive long lines of faithful peasants seeking her blessing, her advice, and even medical attention. This could take hours. The simple medications she offered to the sick she felt could in no way harm them. The combination of her sincere desire to be of service with the deep faith the "patients" had in her therapeutic powers might even have effected some cures along the way.

After leaving Lanchow they made their way to the great monastery of Lhabrang. There any possibility of remaining incognito was out of the question, for there was much visiting between the monasteries of Lhabrang and Kumbum, and she was well known to Tseundup, the wealthy steward of Lhabrang, who gave a magnificent Chinese feast in her honor. It was the traditional repast served on the greatest occasions, begining with desserts, and finishing with soup. Between were many courses comprising meat and fish dishes, many vegetables, and pastas. They sat down at one P.M. and finished after six! She was presented to the recently discovered reincarnation of Jamyang Chedpa, the grand lama of Lhabrang,

who was still a very young child. Seated on a pile of
cushions added to the oversized throne, wearing a heavy
robe and the large hat of his predecessor, the young
tulku performed his ceremonial role with gravity. He
kept his head bowed toward the sacred text in his lap,
which he pretended to be reading. Suddenly, as Alexandra was bowing reverently to present him with her
offerings, he looked her staight in the face and gave her
what she described as a mischievous smile. It lasted but
a moment. Then he reverted to the role he was already
disciplined to play, and solemnly handed her a book
wrapped in yellow silk.

Their departure from Lhabrang was retarded by the
many people who came to bid them farewell, bearing
gifts and offerings. After only a few hours of traveling
they realized night would find them still on the road
unless they stopped in the next village. They had hoped
to be many miles beyond this place, but fatigue had
overtaken them. The servant who was sent to request
lodgings in the nearest house was abruptly refused.
Suddenly, as though awakening from a dream, Yongden
stepped forward and hailed a woman who was regarding
the scene from a window. He asked her where he could
find the home of a certain "Passang." The woman directed them to his dwelling, which was unquestionably
the most elegant in the vicinity. Yongden knocked on the
door and announced in an imperious manner that they
had been sent by Kouchog Leszang of the monastery of
Lhabrang, who commanded the master of the house to
lodge their party in his finest manner. The door was
immediately opened and they were greeted with great
respect. A fine supper was served, after which the entire
family, plus servants, lined up to be blessed in turn by
the khadoma. When finally they had retired to their
sumpuous quarters, Alexandra at last had an opportunity to ask her son how he knew the name of Passang,
and who, in fact was Kouchog Leszang? "I have no idea,"
he replied, "it just suddenly came to me." "You never

heard these people mentioned in Lhabrang?" she insisted. "No, I've racked my brain, but I never heard
them mentioned in Lhabrang or anywhere else. I just
suddenly had the idea to say that. It was absolutely on
impulse."

Well before she was awake the next morning, a long
line of people was waiting with requests for blessings,
divinations, and other magic rites and rituals. She had
no choice but to accede. It was always painful for her.
From the beginning her mission had been to purge
Buddhism of the superstitions, exorcisms, and magic
offices with which it had been overlaid by the faithful of
many generations. While performing with all the solemnity of an archbishop, she still longed to convince them
of the inutility of these practices, to stress how the
Buddha himself had formally condemned them to his
disciples. But she had learned from long experience that
it was useless. Not only would they not believe her, they
would have grave doubts about her own devotion.

Yongden, every bit as skeptical as she, nevertheless
mocked her scruples. His opinion was that blowing on
the back of an elderly rheumatic, or into the ear of one
who was deaf did absolutely no harm and made them
feel much better. He admonished her, as had the
gomchen so many years before, to have compassion on
the poor illiterates who sought her help. And since it was
part of her necessary disguise, all the more reason to
carry it off with authority. Thus she was resigned to
continue her "ecclesiastical functions" wherever they
made a halt.

One woman who had stayed apart during the lengthy
presentation in the home of Passang approached Alexandra timidly after the others had left. Tearfully she
recounted that her father, whom she had greatly loved,
had died a few weeks previously, and she wanted to know
if he had been reborn in a happy circumstance. Alexandra, who never failed to remember the anniversary of
her own father's death, responded to this woman with

deep sympathy. Excusing herself, she retired to her
room, where she sank into profound meditation. Gradually a vision realized itself in her mind. She saw the
interior of an elegant shop, its shelves laden with luxurious objects, silks, precious jade, and enamels. The
place was obviously Chinese. The proprietor, unusually
tall for his race, was attired handsomely in black silk.
Somehow Alexandra "knew" that he had recently become the father of a son. Gradually the scene faded. She
was puzzled by the Chinese "decor" of her vision, as the
young woman in question was Tibetan. Still, she had
followed the procedure that any lama would have undertaken in the circumstances. Returning to the grieving
young woman, she told her that her father had been
reborn into a wealthy merchant's family in the north of
China. She was sure of this because of the size of the
man. He would grow to manhood in a land where the
Buddha was revered. She could cease to be anxious in
his regard. The young woman, though still bearing the
burden of her loss, was greatly relieved.

Yongden, meanwhile, continued to delight in playing
the prankster. He was not above announcing that she
was actually one hundred years old, to the stupefaction
of the assembly, or showing her flashlight to incredulous
souls, claiming that with this instrument, "the precious
joy born of itself," she could start and stop the rain from
falling, destroy crops or render the land fertile, make
animals and people healthy or cause them to die. He was
far less convinced of her superior wisdom than were her
servants, however, and often disputed her decisions.
When she reproached him for this he would say, "I
resemble you more and more!" It was true. The lamas
had often commented that it was their close association
during previous lives that had brought them together.
Between them was forged a bond of understanding that
would withstand all the dangers and mishaps that life
could lay in their path.

As they descended slowly along the mountainous frontier, the conditions of the route became worse and worse. She often commented that she traveled to observe and learn, not to beat a speed record,[4] something of an understatement. She continued to be enchanted in spite of the rugged mountainous terrain, roads washed away by floods, constant fatigue of men and the poor beasts in need of shoeing, and the perilous bridges composed of loose planks held together by ropes they were forced to cross. The spring rains seemed never to cease, soaking Alexandra and her men to the skin. Often it was impossible to lie down at night. She would doze fitfully in her wet garments, and then, when morning arrived, set out courageously, finding that a few hours of walking in the fresh air restored her health and dissipated her fatigue.

This was the life for which she had always yearned— to freely roam the wastelands of the earth, confronting each day's adventure with a cheerful heart and good courage. Nothing seemed capable of derailing her. She drew the line only when her companions wanted to open a coffin they noticed beside the route to see if it contained a femur, an important object of ritual for them. Her reason: Cholera was raging in the area and she feared contagion more than "evil spirits."

But the latter did not leave her alone. One evening she was seated in the kitchen of a farmhouse where an elderly couple had offered them lodging. Her men were occupied with the mules. The old woman was preparing their evening meal. Suddenly a young "idiot" entered the kitchen. Believing him to be one of the caravan, the woman offered him something to eat. Rolling his eyes and drooling, he let it fall to the floor and ran from the room. The poor woman was terrified. She was convinced he was an "evil spirit" attached to the caravan, and no effort on the part of Alexandra could dissuade her. She became hysterical. During the night Yongden awakened Alexandra and informed her that the woman had become very ill. Her husband was convinced that they were responsible for the arrival of the "evil spirit" that had brought on her sickness. If the villagers were alerted, there could be trouble. Quietly they packed their belongings and left before dawn. Later, on the trail, they were informed by a passing messenger that the woman had died. Alexandra was certain that she had died of fright. Later, however, she had an opportunity to consult a learned Tibetan lama who specialized in occult science and magic. He suggested that the "idiot" was possibly a *tulpa* who had escaped the control of the one who had created him. The Tibetans believed that certain initiates had the power to create phantom beings, or tulpas, capable of behaving in the world like natural persons, but having no consciousness of their own. Occasionally such creatures escaped the control of their creators and moved independently in the world.

The small caravan continued to descend through a landscape that might well have inspired a Chinese monochrome painting. Jagged, rocky cliffs rose on either side of the tortuous route they were forced to follow. Twisted evergreens punctuated the distant slopes like so many meditating hermits. And, half concealed by intermittent fog and rain, bizarre shapes loomed before them. Were they the moldering ruins of ancient temples, the disguised forms of not-so-benevolent local deities, or visions produced by the fatigue of those painful hours of climbing and perilous descent? This slow peregrination along the border of Szechuan seemed to carry Alexandra not only outside the context of space as normally she had defined it, but beyond the margins of time as well. The monotonous present seemed to blend with the dreamlike past and the mist-enshrouded future in such a way as to disappear altogether. This "past" was for her not a question of "remembering." It intruded on her present experience and merged with it. As an example of this there was an episode that took place in Mowkow, as they were installing themselves in an inn. As her servants were discharging the mules in the enclosed courtyard, several men who had been loitering in the street came forward to help, as was customary, hoping to receive a generous tip. As Yongden was distributing this money from a large bag of coins resting beside him, one of the men, who had been regarding the money with a fixed, hypnotic expression, darted forward and thrust his hand into the bag. He was of course pounced upon by the other men, and thrown out of the courtyard into the street, where he nevertheless remained, heedless of repeated threats, gazing longingly into the courtyard at the money he desired so desperately. Alexandra, observing this man, was suddenly transported to another time and place, when in mid-winter she had camped on the steppes. A solitary, half-starved wolf had appeared near the camp, circling the enclosure, watching the tethered horses with hungry eyes. From long experience, he understood the meaning of the tents, that strange creatures bearing "exploding sticks" were part of this scene, yet was so hypnotized by the presence of food that he could not bring himself to leave the camp. Finally, Alexandra could stand it no longer. Taking a large piece of meat (which they could ill afford to sacrifice), she approached the wolf and threw it in his direction. He grabbed the prize and disappeared with it in his mouth. At Mowkow, the baggage had been unloaded and her men had gone in search of dinner. The Chinese "thief" remained transfixed before the entrance of the inn. Quietly Alexandra removed a large coin from her pocket and threw it in his direction. Like the hungry wolf, he pounced as it rolled in the dust and was out of sight. Two "thieves," two hungry creatures, and two offerings had coalesced in a moment's clear awareness. To play the role of judge in our chaotic world seemed absurd to Alexandra. The best morality for "us poor human beings" she felt, was to give each other the alms of our mutual pity.[5] For Alexandra the concept of "justice" was often relative.

In Tsakalo they were forced to wait some time for the saddle sores of the mules to heal. Fortunately there were agreeable accommodations in a fairly new inn. The rooms in which Yongden and Alexandra passed the long hours absorbed in reading gave onto a balcony, where the curious would frequently pass by to regard the strange dame-lama as she studied her texts. One day a tall, well-dressed lama with gray hair entered her room, without so much as knocking, and insisted on talking with her. Always nervous about giving away her identity, Alexandra did not welcome this intrusion, but she tried to make light of it, so as not to arouse suspicion. This unexpected visitor had an unusual presence, difficult to ignore. He questioned her at length about herself and Yongden, their country of origin, where they had lived, and their motives for adopting the religious life. He then intensified his discourse with a moving commentary on the sad condition of this present world, in which men were completely obsessed with the demands of their own egos, and the tremendous need for committed teachers to expound the doctrine. Referring suddenly to Yongden, he observed that he was a tulku. Alexandra asked him how he had known this. He replied, "One can sense it even if he is not officially recognized. He will have an unusual life." He offered to share with Yongden the teaching he had received from his own master, and invited him to visit him in his quarters in the nearby monastery. For the remainder of their stay Yongden visited him every day. His importance as a man of letters was evident, and great respect was shown him by the other monks. As she pored over her texts, Alexandra mused that Yongden's "unusual life" had indeed already begun. The strange lama's penetrating mind had apparently seen through their disguise.

The other incident of this place that made a lasting impression on Alexandra was the daily ritual of lamentation made by the owner of the inn before the open doorway of a room facing on the courtyard, in which her son was dying of tuberculosis. Every evening she placed herself there, accompanied only by an indifferent boy, whose function was to repeat certain prescribed chants in accompaniment to her heartrending pleas to the deity whom she implored to save her child. People came and went in the courtyard, conducting business as usual, totally oblivious to her anguish. It was as though she did not exist for them, and the agonized woman remained totally isolated, surrounded by the cruel indifference of the world. Alexandra was asked to visit the young man, who obviously had very little time to live. She advised the mother to bring him out of his dark, airless room into the sunshine as long as his condition permitted. There was little else she could suggest, but the memory of the mother's agony continued to haunt her.

Although the sores on their beasts had not completely healed, they were able to engage a local muleteer and extra animals to continue on their way. So they moved on, covering at least twenty-five miles each day, through the dense forests that covered the almost perpendicular slopes of this mountainous country. Under intermittent rain, they ascended to one dramatic pass at fifteen thousand feet. When finally they arrived at the base, the muleteer was eager to continue the rest of the way with them. Alexandra, always conscious of the need for economy, decided that her own beasts were well enough to dispense with this added expense, and let him go. She always wondered whether it was this disgruntled man who made known to the Chinese authorities that they were in the vicinity. As she and Yongden crossed the village of Foupien she understood a functionary's remark to the man beside him, "They are Europeans."

They camped outside the town in a beautiful cemetery, beside which there was ample pasture for the mules. The following day they were accosted by two Chinese administrators who demanded to see their papers and to inspect their baggage. Noting that Yongden's bag contained some money, they held him, saying that Alexandra and the others were free to leave. She of course refused, and threatened to contact the French and English consuls at Chengtu (which was several days' journey

away). It was clear the administrator did not relish
trouble from this quarter, but there was always the
question of "face." Alexandra finally made it easier for
him by showing him some papers, in a language he could
not possibly understand, having nothing to do with their
permission to travel. He was delighted to be let off the
hook so easily. If only he had seen them before! He
apologized for his mistake. He had taken Yongden for a
Japanese. They were free to go on their way. Since by
then it was too late in the day for them to depart,
Alexandra demanded that he send them their evening
meal. A copious repast was delivered to them by the
administrator's servants. In that way, once again every-
body saved face. Manipulating events so as to arrange
for this was a continuing challenge.

As they set out for Mowkong, however, Alexandra
realized that the chances of moving toward Lhasa without being recognized were virtually nonexistent. To dis-
miss her servants and sell her animals would arouse
suspicion on the part of both the Chinese and Tibetan
authorities, so she could only continue the route she had
originally planned. It led to Mowkow Ting, where a
French Catholic missionary, Father Charrier, having
been advised of her arrival by the Chinese administrator, had prepared comfortable lodgings for her in a
school building that was as yet not in use. The priest was
delighted to have an intelligent visitor with whom he
could speak his own language, and urged her to remain
as long as she wished, which gave her an opportunity to
reflect on her difficult and uncertain position before
moving on. In spite of Alexandra's deep distrust of
Catholicism, she was always warmly received by the
clergy she encountered in Asia. None of them tried to
dissuade her from her "heresy." Instead they were
charmed by her erudite conversation, and often pressed
unwanted gifts on her, such as meat and game (they were
often enthusiastic hunters) and rare wine and beer. She

deeply appreciated the refuge she obtained in the missions in this desolate region.

After much reflection she decided her only course was to continue on and hope for the best. But the omens were bad. The weather worsened. Bridges were wiped out and roads flooded. There were situations when even their lives seemed in danger. In one difficult place a horse belonging to one of their traveling companions fell from a cliff and was killed outright. The next morning her already terrified servants awoke to find that the owner of the unfortunate animal had skinned it (such hides were valuable) and draped the gory object in front of their camp. This was indeed the last straw. The young men fled. Yongden, always clever at dealing with such crises, found immediate replacements. Later the contrite young Tibetans returned. But she had decided that Sotar, the one who was most voluble, often spreading information she hoped to keep secret, might as well return to his home in Sinin. Little by little she must reduce her too visible entourage. It seemed prudent for the time being to give up her efforts to join any of the caravan routes to Lhasa, so she made plans to visit the neighboring country of Kham. This had its inevitable effect on her fragile digestion. She had heard about an American doctor who was in charge of a hospital at Batang, not far across the Tibetan frontier from Kanze. Armed with a dossier of official papers from a local Chinese mandarin, she took off. But she had not traveled very far on the other side of the Tibetan frontier before she was stopped by an administrator straight out of a musical comedy, complete with flags and trumpets, who announced haughtily that her Chinese papers weren't even fit to spit on. There ensued an encounter that later, she could appreciate as hilarious theater. She threatened suicide, assassination, or the two in combination. Ordered to retrace her steps, she obstinately refused, to the delight and admiration of her entourage. La Diva was playing her favorite role with such gusto that she even broke her baton in half across the back of one unfortunate who attempted to physically detain her. Finally her persecutors gave up and allowed her to proceed in the direction of Jakyendo in peace. By the time she arrived in this remote outpost, fall was approaching. She had conceived a plan to return northward in full circle, to the region of Koko Nor, but it was obvious that winter would find her in the midst of the great desert. There seemed to be no choice but to winter in Jakyendo. After a short time in this inhospitable, dreary city, she suffered an attack of what could only be described as cabin fever. They must somehow leave, regardless of weather or other difficult circumstances. Perhaps they could move toward the south and try to find a more agreeable place to spend the winter. This ill-considered excursion almost ended in disaster. Ultimately blocked from going any further by heavy snows, they were forced to return to Jakyendo. There the gods favored her at last. The winter she had so dreaded turned out to be the mildest in years. During this time she had ample opportunity to reflect. She knew that the Tibetan authorities had been alerted to her efforts to enter the country. The only way she would ever succeed was to disappear for a time and try again much later in an entirely different way. In the interval she hoped the authorities would have their hands full of more pressing irritations and would forget all about her. The best place in which to become invisible lay to the north. She had always longed to visit the Gobi Desert and the famous temple-grotto of a thousand buddhas. It was a region that was completely uncharted on the maps—what greater temptation for Alexandra! Outfitting her somewhat reduced caravan with the little money she had left, she headed north toward Koko Nor.

The winter of 1922 overtook the group at Kanchow, not too far to the north of Koko Nor. There, again prevented by the weather from going further, Alexandra undertook to complete a work, the "Tibetan Iliad" so dear to her heart, that she had been working on from time to time. Finally published under the title of *The Superhuman Life of Gesar of Ling*,[6] it recounts the adventurous life of one of Tibet's best-loved traditional heroes. She also sent a number of articles to Mouchy, destined for *Mercure*. Sitting in her freezing room, heated only occasionally when a little coal could be obtained, she continued to work, oblivious to any discomfort.

The small caravan now possessed only five animals. In Sinin she had encountered the talkative Sotar and had reengaged him. During these long winter months in Kanchow, on the edge of the vast emptiness of the Gobi, Alexandra continued to philosophize for the benefit of her distant husband. She remarked that since the war had overturned a world which wasn't exactly spectacular even before, there was no reason to be crushed by the new world and play the role of victim in the midst of all the "fox-trotting fools."[7]

Mouchy was advised to keep all her old operatic costumes, from which she planned to create "original" skirts and blouses when she returned. There was a final, optimistic quotation: "He who possesses savoir faire is capable of being at ease even in hell."[8]

A group of Russian immigrants, one of them a doctor, arrived in Kanchow with eight children. They had crossed Siberia and Mongolia seeking refuge from the revolution in their own country. Their presence provided a touch of "European culture," in this remote place. It may have been some conversation with them that inspired Alexandra to observe: "In Europe, poverty, or even reduced means, forces one to endure a repugnant promiscuity with common people. . . . A 'lady' prefers to maintain a certain distance . . . a perfectly legitimate desire even among the most sincere democrats and socialists."[9]

In mid-February, in spite of the extreme cold, she decided to leave for Tungwham to see the long-anticipated "thousand buddhas" carved in the sandstone cliffs. The country she traversed reminded her of the deserts of North Africa. They arose at three A.M. and spent all day in the saddle, crossing the endless dunes. After such days she admitted to being "a little tired." Once again they were forced to sleep on *kangs*, the heated platforms of northern China and Mongolia, where one was roasted on one side and frozen on the other.

With the arrival of spring, they retraced their steps and arrived in Lanchow, where at last she received a letter from Mouchy, the first in a long time. While there, she arranged to send a large number of parcels to her bank in Shanghai, eliminating all but the absolute necessities. Then they began to descend a route somewhat parallel to that they had followed two years earlier, except that it traversed a more arid country that was excruciatingly hot during the day and freezing at night. She had gradually let her servants go. Only the horse and her great black mule remained to transport her reduced baggage. At the end of May they arrived in Kwangyuan, where they were welcomed in the Catholic mission by a Chinese priest. Since he spoke no French they tried to communicate in Latin, at which Alexandra was apparently adept enough to arrange the sale of her beloved great black mule for a good price. She was pleased to leave her faithful beast, who had carried her over so many miles, in an opulent stable where he would be well treated, and mounted only on important occasions by the priest, a reluctant equestrian.

On and on they followed the route, plagued by the intense heat, the hordes of mosquitoes, and contaminated water that gave them both dysentery. Alexandra was finally forced to enter the French hospital in Chengta, from which she was sent to the home of the director of the Pasteur Institute, with instructions to remain there and rest, advice that never carried much weight with Alexandra. Her social life in Chengta had a certain variety, however. The French consul introduced her to the local Catholic bishop, Monseigneur Rouchousse, who entertained them lavishly with coffee, elegant pastries, and even offered them cigarettes. He reflected what a shame it was that Alexandra didn't "work for them," that she would have made a wonderful missionary—so many converts!

War had once again erupted along the Sino-Tibetan frontier. The route to Batang, where, once again, she hoped to consult the American doctor, was impassable. She would have to follow another route. The consul insisted on lending her money against her account in Shanghai, which she could withdraw as needed at the Catholic missions en route. For the first time she even carried a French flag as protection against being fired upon in the battle zones she would be obliged to cross. Although she continued to be plagued by illness, she was able to attain the summit of the sacred mountain at Omishan in the midst of a great crowd of pilgrims that moved methodically from temple to temple. This pressing mob, plus the odors emanating from the open latrines along the way, nauseated her.

Still they continued to descend through the war-torn country, finding little to eat, staying wherever possible in Catholic missions. She became weaker and weaker, yet crossed the Mekong River suspended from a cable without incident. Finally they arrived at the home of Father Ouvrard, a relative of Clemenceau. The presence of another guest, an American botanist working for the Washington Geographic Society, caused her to extend her visit. She was fearful that he might insist on accompanying them, so she waited until he had departed. She told Mouchy to keep the letter of Father Ouvrard, which would show that she had passed that way on October 23, 1923.[10]

12

Footprints on the Wind

«1923–1924»

The word "pilgrimage" is heavy with meaning. It evokes a flood of images, historic, religious, political, and aesthetic: Mecca, Gethsemane, Omaha Beach, Bayreuth, Red Square, Gettysburg, Santiago da Compostella, the Knights Templar, the piercing shrieks of Moslem fanatics, and the long line of wheelchairs that moves every day toward the grotto of Lourdes. Relics indicate that long before the Christian era routes of pilgrimage crossed the European continent, punctuated by the menhirs and dolmens that still survive. The journey, often on foot and covering excruciatingly difficult terrain, toward a distant and significant goal, is burdened with the primordial symbolism of our passage from birth to death. Pilgrimages, whether consciously or unconsciously achieved, make explicit the fulfillment of our human destiny.

When Alexandra left the mission of Father Ouvrard on the morning of October 24, 1923, to set forth on her own long-contemplated pilgrimage, it was in complete awareness that she had embarked on a significant journey. If ever there was an examined life, it was that of Alexandra David-Néel. From a religious point of view, Lhasa was not of overwhelming importance to her. She viewed the Potala, and its *proprietaire*, the Dalai Lama, with the French republican skepticism she never abandoned. Bodh-Gaya, that most sacred of sites, she had visited when she was in India. As a devout Buddhist she had no need to prostrate herself before the Potala. Her obsession with reaching Lhasa by whatever means far transcended religious or philosophic considerations. On one level she was intrigued by the mystery that seemed to envelop the Forbidden City, but on another she wanted to right a "wrong"—the grave injustice inflicted on "her" village of Lachen in Sikkim and "her" gomchen by the British authorities in retaliation for her trip to Shigatse in 1916. And she must have desired aesthetic closure as well. She was an artist who had created out of her life a chef d'oeuvre. As far as she was concerned this was the last act of her great performance, and the last act required a climax. On the first night after her departure, as she gazed at the summit of Kha Karpo[1] gleaming in the moonlight, she formulated the raison d'être of this supremely defiant gesture.

"Stop here! Do not go any further!"[2] With this irrational command a handful of administrators, throughout history, have prevented explorers and scientists from advancing the knowledge of the world. All those who, like Galileo, Columbus, and Marco Polo, had defied the constraints of physical and intellectual barriers were her silent witnesses as she swore to herself: "You cannot pass! Really? A woman will pass."[3]

A woman will pass. A woman, no longer young, with a delicate constitution and bleeding feet, but possessed of an indomitable will and a refusal to accept defeat. This woman will pass. Alexandra realized that the moment had arrived when she would establish her position in history. She must retrieve the gauntlet life had thrown down before her. No power on earth would bar her way. Not only would she pass, but by a route no one before had ever attempted.[4]

The first difficulty was to get rid of the porters who accompanied them on their "brief expedition into the mountains to gather plant specimens." To have left without them would have immediately aroused suspicion, though it was clear Father Ouvrard was not deceived as to the true nature of their outing. (The presence of an American botanist in the vicinity made this a plausible explanation. They would simply be considered part of his group.) One of the men she commanded to go gather wood for the camp fire. The other she discharged, explaining that her swollen, bleeding feet required that she rest for a week at least, and she no longer needed two porters. He left, enchanted with his generous tip, assuming that his companion would be retained to see to her needs. When the wood gatherer returned she told him the same story, but gave him a letter to post in the next village, thereby insuring that he would return by a different route than his colleague. It would be days before they encountered each other and exchanged stories. By then she and Yongden would, she hoped, have melted into the multitude of pilgrims who traveled the roads of Tibet.

Suddenly they were alone. The plan they had discussed evening after evening during the two long years they had circled the mountains and deserts of Central Asia was at last being realized. So overwhelmed were they that for a time they could only look at each other in silence. As night began to fall they set out. The packs they carried, containing only the minimum necessities (one caldron, two bowls, two spoons, one knife, chopsticks, tsampa, tea, leather to resole their boots, extra thongs, and a minuscule tent), were still extremely heavy. Alexandra had not lied about her feet.

The path they were obliged to follow in order to reach the pilgrimage route was incredibly steep. Several times in the darkness they took the wrong turn and had to retrace their steps. But at last, as day was breaking, they had reached a point where they were no longer visible from the village below and could crawl into the protection of the undergrowth for the sleep they desperately needed. Their Chinese garments were abandoned, and they emerged as a Tibetan lama and his aged mother making a religious journey. She had not been able to procure a real Tibetan bonnet, so she strapped a length of fabric around her head, simulating a turban. She had blackened her brown hair with Chinese ink and "lengthened" it with the aid of a yak's tail. Her already bronzed face and hands she darkened with soot wiped from the bottom of the caldron. This completed her disguise.

It was decided that, whenever possible, they would travel by night and sleep during the day. The less they were observed, the better. And after one narrow escape when they were overtaken as they were conversing in English, they spoke only Tibetan, even when they were certain to be quite alone. They had fabricated a very believable "history." They were natives of Amdo, a relatively distant district they knew very well, and bore the heat of midday with difficulty. It was for this reason, in case they were questioned, that they traveled at night. (And indeed this was demanded of them the very first time they encountered anyone on the route. The Tibetans were unfortunately extremely curious and talkative.)

A major problem was the scarcity of water. They didn't dare risk carrying anything "strange" that would arouse suspicion, so the famous thermos had been reluctantly abandoned. The hot-water bottle that might have served to carry a small supply remained buried at the bottom of one of the packs for a long time. At times they suffered terribly from thirst. But no discomfort, difficulty, or anxiety could diminish the euphoria in which Alexandra moved: She felt those to be the happiest days she had ever lived.[5]

The joy was always accompanied by an undercurrent of worry, and the danger of discovery, especially during the first weeks. One of the first times she allowed herself to fall into a deep slumber, she awoke with a start to find a Tibetan soldier watching her gravely, from a few meters away. She froze with terror. Then, to protect her disguise, she performed the most "Tibetan" gesture she could imagine. Although it filled her with repugnance, she blew her nose on her fingers. The sacrifice was wasted. As her eyes began to focus on the soldier she became aware that "he" was nothing more than a large upright wedge of stone.

Such mirages were a frequent experience. One night they could see the campfire of other travelers on a ledge just above them on the mountain. A careful examination of the site the following morning revealed absolutely no evidence of any fire. These mysterious illuminations in the forest at night became so commonplace they ceased even to pay attention to them. One morning, however, when they had continued to walk later than usual, they both were astonished to see on the riverbank opposed to them a charming village, though none was indicated on their detailed map. It was composed of beautiful villas and elegant miniature chateaux. There was no sign that they were inhabited, and the only sound emanating from the place was the muted tinkling of what sounded like a silver carillon. Not wishing to risk being seen, they left the riverbank and camped high up on the mountain, postponing until evening their examination of this unusual place. When they descended to the river that evening they searched in vain for the beautiful little village. It had completely disappeared. Finally Alexandra was forced to acknowledge that in their state of deep fatigue they must have "dreamed" the entire event. They had, in fact, seen nothing there when they had arrived in the morning, but had experienced the whole thing in their sleep during the day. It had perhaps been one of those "communal dreams" of individuals who are in close rapport. Yongden, however, remembered that while they were admiring the sight of this place that exuded such abnormal fascination he had scratched a magic symbol with the metal tip of his staff on the flat surface of a stone beside the path, in order to prevent any mischievous god or demon from interfering with their progress. It took him only a moment of searching to locate the stone with the image still clearly visible. He observed, with an enigmatic smile, "It had the effect of making the 'village' created to enchant us disappear."

The great forests through which they traveled were inhabited by many wild animals. They saw them from time to time, and one night Alexandra awoke to find herself face to face with a leopard. "Little friend," she murmured softly, so as not to awaken Yongden, "I have been close to a greater prince of the jungle than you. Be on your way quietly."[6] Solitary wolves crossed their route from time to time and paid them little attention.

Their first high pass was the col of Dokar, at 16,500 feet. The summit was decorated by many altars and flags of all colors, with myriad inscriptions. A blast of frigid air greeted them as they arrived. Nevertheless they followed the ritual of turning to face the four cardinal points and declaring, "May all beings find happiness," before beginning the steep descent, which they accomplished, not without difficulty, in the first severe snowstorm they had encountered.

Their custom, like those of other travelers forced to sleep in the open, was to lie with their belongings squeezed between them, their money belts sometimes buried nearby or hidden under their robes. The tiny tent they spread over their outstretched bodies, and when it was covered by a layer of snow they resembled only another patch of white in the forest. Once, however, they were noticed by two men who passed on the route, whom they overheard, discussing whether the "patch" was a man asleep or merely the snow. Yongden, the eternal wag, could not resist responding in a deep, sepulchral tone, "It's the snow."[7] He then arose and engaged them in conversation, while Alexandra remained hidden.

In his capacity as lama, Yongden often was asked to perform various rites and divinations. He did this so well that their route was frequently barred by enthusiastic crowds, and Alexandra would be forced to resort to the "signal" they had devised, by exclaiming, "Karmapa

kieno!" which in their private language meant, "Let's
get out of here immediately!" At other times she assisted
his performance by chanting vigorously. Her talent for
psalmody increased with time, as she became more con-
fident of their safety. She began to enjoy these performances, and brought all her operatic expertise to bear on
the rendition. She enjoyed the opportunity to resurrect
her theatrical repertoire, and only occasionally did she
fall out of character. On one such occasion, when she
became entranced gazing at a magnificent view, something no genuine Tibetan peasant would ever do, Yongden merely said to the puzzled assembly, "Mother is
with the gods." He always included in his discourse a
simple commentary on the true Buddhist doctrine and,
when it was in answer to a request for "healing," he
interjected advice on matters of cleanliness and hygiene.
On one occasion when he was approached to exorcise the
"demon" that was causing a young girl's feet to swell,
thus hindering the progress of her companions, he devised a long, complicated set of rituals that were to be
effected when next they came upon a *chorten*.[8] This was
to last for three days, and the participation of the entire
group was necessary. It would ensure that the poor
young woman could have the rest she so badly needed.
Later, Yongden and Alexandra found the group encir-
cling the chorten he had "predicted" they would find,
ecstatically chanting the required formula. The "demon's" hold on the young woman seemed already to have
diminished. Her feet were improving. He gave his mother
full credit for inspiring in him a talent for inventing such
charitable ruses. Many were the times when their ability
to play the comedy saved a delicate situation. Whenever
they were in danger of being too closely questioned or
examined, one of them would extract an "act" from their
bag of tricks and distract the assembly. Alexandra's
favorite was to begin circulating in the crowd, whining
for alms. She included elaborations as the situation
demanded, narrating a long list of miseries they had

endured, and promising that blessings and good fortune would favor those who were most generous.

The time finally arrived when circumstances forced them to accept a pressing invitation to spend the night in a peasant's home. This required sitting on a floor covered with the remnants of food, rancid butter, grease, and spit deposited there by a large family, and accepting pieces of meat that a civilized dog might well refuse, served on the corner of the hostess's filthy apron. One of the more impressive performances of her entire career was played out before an almost "empty house" when she retired discreetly to the roof to accomplish her needs, leaning out over the edge as was required. Over the rigorous objections of Yongden, two rugged male members of the household rushed to her aid and insisted that they hold her on either side to make sure she did not tumble backward into the pit below.

One memorable day they had paused to make tea beside the road before ascending a particularly difficult mountain. For some reason, Yongden began to build their fire on the flat rocks of the partially dry river bed. At this moment a very young child ran toward him and prostrated himself with great ceremony. He told them that his grandfather, in a house nearby, was on the point of death. For days he had asked members of the family to keep watch in that particular place because "his" personal lama would soon arrive to accomplish the final rites. The lama could be recognized by the fact that he would build a fire in the riverbed itself, rather than in the usual place on the bank. Alexandra and Yongden, eager to continue on their way before the day had advanced any further, did their best to convince the child that he had made a mistake. Suddenly he was joined by an older child, who confirmed the story and was even more insistent. At last, in order to convince the family of this obvious error, they agreed to visit the home of the dying man. When they arrived, the man, who did not seem to be moribund, tried to rise from his bed to prostrate himself with joy, but Yongden insisted that he dispense with this ritual. "His" long-awaited lama had at last arrived. Yongden was most reluctant to perform the office, as the man really did not appear to be on the brink of death. He tried, rather, to exhort him to make an effort to regain his strength. But the man was adamant. He claimed he had kept himself alive only because he was sure his lama would not fail to arrive in time. Reluctantly Yongden began to chant the office of the *bardo*[9] as the large and devoted family watched with rapture. When he had finished, the man lay on the bed calmly, his face serene, his eyes filled with a transcendent light. They decided it was too late to begin the difficult ascent that lay before them, and accepted an invitation to spend the night. They made their start well before the sun arose, and had progressed a distance on their way when a member of the family overtook them on the route to inform them that, even as they had left the village in the early dawn, the old man had sighed quietly and expired in peace.

The Tibetans' lives were circumscribed by innumerable superstitions, one of which required that if one's hat had blown off, to retrieve it risked courting all kinds of misfortune. One day Yongden saw a woman's hat fabricated of filthy sheepskin in the path. Spearing it with the point of his staff, he tossed it aside. But Alexandra, impelled by some intuition, picked it up. Yongden chided her, saying this was even worse than picking up one's own hat that had fallen, but she persisted in keeping it nonetheless. One day she washed it thoroughly and attached it to her pack. As they moved deeper into the country, and her turban began to attract the kind of attentive curiosity they were always eager to avoid, she discarded the length of cloth and donned her sheepskin "chapeau." All comments about her headgear immediately ceased. Not only did it improve her disguise, but it undoubtedly prevented her from catching cold in the high passes they repeatedly ascended.

Disguise was always a problem. One day in the home of a peasant, they were given warm milk and tsampa, which it was necessary to mix together with the fingers. She had recently blackened her hair and her hands were still covered with ink. To her horror she suddenly noticed that the milk was decorated with black streaks. Yongden also noticed this, and whispered to her, "Drink it at once!" If her hostess were to notice, there would be much questioning. Closing her eyes, she downed the nauseating mixture in a gulp.

What was most exhausting and even painful in her existence was the role she was constantly obliged to play in order not to give away her incognito.[10] It required that she be constantly on guard. To avoid contact with the curious and talkative natives among whom they were forced to spend a certain amount of time, they sometimes left the main route and followed more difficult, but more isolated, alternative itineraries.

The time arrived when they would have to make a choice of the route by which they would approach Lhasa. During the winter she had spent in Jakyendo, Alexandra had as her nearest neighbor the British explorer and geographer Sir George Pereira, who was on official visit to the Dalai Lama. He was quite willing to show Alexandra his many maps, and even allowed her to copy several.[11] One day after tea when they were looking at the map of Tibet, he pointed his finger to the route that followed the supposed course of the river Poulong Tsangpo. He commented that it would be an interesting route by which to arrive at Lhasa, but no one as far as he knew had ever gone that way. His remark made a great impression on Alexandra. She had heard the many "histoires" concerning the inhabitants of the Po country. They were redoubtable warriors, it was said, and it had long been rumored that they were cannibals. This did not in any way intimidate Alexandra. The thought of traversing a region hitherto unexplored was too much of a temptation to refuse. It was decided that this was the route they would take. There was the advantage of their being removed for a time from the constant surveillance of their kind-hearted but curious companions of the route. Winter was already upon them. Many of the passes would soon be blocked by heavy snow. They would be forced to traverse a region composed of two ranges separated by a wide valley. If, having crossed the first range, it snowed behind them, and they found the second pass of Aigni closed, they would undoubtedly perish long before they were discovered. It was a danger to be seriously considered, but the possible rewards outweighed the risks. Also of scientific interest would be the opportunity to determine where exactly the Poulong Tsangpo originated.

They celebrated their decision by indulging in an elegant lunch, beginning with the soup and ending with tea, the reverse of the order in Tibet. The soup consisted of one small square of bacon cut in minuscule pieces dancing in a caldron of boiling water, to which had been added a little flour.

"The soup you have prepared is delicious."

"I must agree."

"My dogs would have refused to swallow it."[12]

And they were off.

They spent the first night in a small, deserted shepherd's cabin, where a quantity of dried manure served them well for fuel. In spite of the intense cold, Alexandra wandered for some time under the light of a brilliant full moon, "savoring the delights of the solitude and calm," as described in the Buddhist scripture.[13]

Late the following day they noticed a small monument such as Tibetans fabricated to mark the summit of a pass. They rejoiced to know they had almost achieved the first challenge, but arrived to find only a long valley leading on and on ahead of them. When they first attained the next elevation they stopped in a mixture of admiration and horror. Ahead of them extended a white immensity of heavy snow, a plateau that rose very grad-

ually, at the end of which was a vertical wall of glaciers
and scintillating peaks. There was nothing to indicate
where the route was buried under the deep snow. The
day was already well advanced. If they made a mistake
of even a few feet it would mean their wandering the
entire night in this glacial wilderness. After surveying
the scene long and carefully in silence, the innate wisdom
of the explorer said to Alexandra that they should
continue in a straight line forward. As she was less
burdened than Yongden and was eager to discover some
sign indicating they were on the route, she pressed her
steps, and moved on up ahead. At one point she turned
to see if he was catching up with her. There, alone in a
vast white wilderness stretching as far as the eye could
see, was a tiny black dot, moving very, very slowly. She
was suddenly confronted by the enormity of her responsibility. She had brought him here, this faithful companion of so many adventures, a young man on the very
brink of life. She thought of the frozen corpses so often
found in the high mountain passes of the Himalayas. A
death that she might find altogether appropriate would
be inadmissible for him. Somehow they must prevail. She
increased her pace up and every upward as the day was
coming to an end. Suddenly she perceived ahead of her
a small mound from which bits of frozen cloths crackled
in the wind. She had achieved the pass! She waved her
arms wildly in the direction of the speck in the snow,
which seemed to have fallen even further behind. He
didn't seem to see her. She continued to signal. Finally
he waved his baton in reply and, as if encouraged,
hastened his steps. As she waited beside the cairn that
marked the pass of Deon, the moon rose, creating a
world of enchantment and mystery such as she had never
seen. Murmuring sounds carried on the wind signaled
that the guardians of this great unknown region were
perhaps in council. Would these intruders from another
world be allowed to pass?

They continued walking through the night, their energy renewed by the knowledge that they were on the right path. On the other side, it was easier to perceive the route because there was less snow. Although they had not stopped once, nor taken any nourishment during nineteen hours, Alexandra did not feel tired. But suddenly she experienced an almost overwhelming need to sleep, and they decided to make camp in a sheltered area. A fire was imperative. After gathering some dried yak dung and arranging it in a small heap, Yongden withdrew the flint from his belt and tried to strike a spark. Nothing happened. During the long hours of wading through heavy snow, the flint had become damp. What would they do? Suddenly Yongden reminded his mother of the training in tumo she had received during the months of her apprenticeship with the gomchen of Lachen. Could she still do this? She told him to continue looking for fuel, which would keep him moving, and taking the flint lay it under her robe next to her skin. She began to concentrate. Soon she had the sensation of flames rising within her. She had not forgotten. By the time Yongden returned with additional fuel, a small fire was burning. The heat of tumo had indeed dried the flint. Yongden looked at her with admiration. Her face was still flushed and her eyes shone with an intense brilliance. But she merely indicated a need for some hot tea.

Near the end of the following day they discovered a small community of shepherds living in the deep valley between the two passes, where even in winter there was pasture enough to sustain the hardy yaks. They persuaded one of these men to accompany them to the next summit with a horse. Alexandra and Yongden rode the animal in turn, to conserve their strength, and the man carried their sacks. In exchange for this service the man refused any remuneration, but requested that the lama perform the necessary rite to bring on the long-delayed snow, as they had suffered an extremely dry season. This Yongden was willing to do, but made it clear that there would be dire retribution on the part of the deities concerned if the formula he left was implemented before they had time to pass well beyond the summit. It worked only too well. As they began to descend from the pass of Aigni, snow started to fall. Before long a veil of white concealed the surrounding country. In spite of this and their diminishing supply of food, Alexandra was determined to search for the source of the Poulong Tsangpo, which required a slight detour. Suddenly there was a cry behind her. Yongden had slipped on a patch of ice concealed by the snow, and had fallen into a crevice. When he attempted to rise to his feet, he turned white and fell back in agony. Quickly Alexandra dropped down beside him and examined his leg. There was no fracture, but the ankle was badly sprained, and it was impossible for him to put any weight on it.

The next few days called on all the reserves of physical and spiritual strength they possessed. They remained in a cave where, happily, they had found refuge, but there was no fuel. Outside, the snow fell and fell. All their meager supply of food had been consumed. Finally Yongden felt he could walk a little with the help of a rude crutch they had made. Slowly, very slowly, they began the descent toward what they hoped would be an inhabited region. But several times they became lost in the whiteness of the snow that never ceased to fall. Yongden became feverish and delirious, and it was all Alexandra could do to prevent his rushing off into the storm. At last they encountered a shepherd's summer cabin, which provided fuel and a chance to resole their boots, which were in shreds. This promised to be a long, difficult process. They melted snow so that at least they would have hot water to drink. Suddenly Yongden had the inspiration to add to the boiling water the trimmings from the leather they had used to cut out soles for their boots. This "soup" provided their Christmas celebration. It was December 25, 1923.

The snow continued to fall steadily. They lost track of

the time. Although Yongden's ankle began to improve, their progress was very slow, and they were very weak from the long fast. But one afternoon, approaching a cabin where they hoped to rest for a while, they were astonished to see a man standing in the doorway. They had encountered their first Popa.

Inside, a dozen men were gathered around a blazing fire. When they heard that the two visitors had descended the Aigni pass they were astounded. It had been completely blocked by snow for days. The Popas viewed the two with great respect, deciding they must enjoy the protection of some very powerful divinities. As they had already finished their repast, no tsampa was left, but the strong buttered tea was the most delicious brew Alexandra and Yongden had ever swallowed.

As they continued through the country of the Popas and repeated the story of their traversing the pass of Aigni, they were welcomed with great admiration. Alexandra's incognito was secure at last. No stranger could have possibly accomplished such a feat. As for the rumors of cannibalism, they had nothing to fear: They were by this time reduced to skin and bones.

The route continued through a dreamlike landscape. In the virgin forest reigned a mysterious obscurity, broken occasionally by clearings from which they glimpsed snow-covered peaks gleaming in the sun against a sky that was a deep royal blue in color. All this they regarded with mute ecstasy, feeling they had attained the limit of the world of men and were approaching that of the gods. In one lush valley the temperature was so mild that Alexandra picked a bough on which grew a cluster of orchids. The very fact of having accomplished such an incredible exercise gave them renewed energy. They were aware that they traveled where no European had ever set foot.

The feared Popas were on the whole kind and welcoming, and those who offered them hospitality gave Alexandra an opportunity to examine at close range the

customs of this rarely visited region of Tibet. There were
several exceptions, however. Twice they encountered
thieves. The first occasion involved two men, who started
to make off with the tent and the two spoons. For the
first time the pistol appeared and was fired well above
the head of one man; it terrified them and they promptly
fled. The second incident was far more dangerous. Seven
men, armed with sabers and knives, began by lifting two
coins from Yongden. They obviously meant to make for
the packs. Alexandra reacted without hesitation. She
began screaming and intoning in turn. The coins had
been given as alms to her son for performing funeral
rites. They were all the couple possessed. Surely the
spirit of the defunct would revenge himself on the thieves
who had committed such a sacrilege. She then invoked a
complete pantheon of terrible divinities against the men.
So terrified were they by this threatening performance
that they threw down the money and prostrated themselves before the lama, imploring his forgiveness. Although Alexandra might deplore the superstitious nature
of the Tibetans, she was not above taking advantage
of it.

Only once on the entire voyage was she "recognized."
One night as they sat in the deep forest by their campfire, a hermit suddenly appeared, carrying nothing but
a staff mounted with a trident. Silently he seated himself
and finally withdrew from his robe a cup formed from a
human skull in which he accepted their offering of tea.
He looked at Alexandra with sharp, penetrating eyes
and asked her why she had discarded her religious robes
and initiation rings. She was overwhelmed. The man
asked Yongden to leave them alone. He then told Alexandra that it was useless to try to remember where they
had met. He told her that he wore many faces and this
one she had never seen.[14] They then discussed at length
many philosophic subjects. The hours passed. At last he
arose and disappeared in the night as silently as he had
come. She said to Yongden, by way of explanation, that

although it was clear the man had recognized them, he would say nothing to anyone about it.

A few nights later she was accosted in a dream by another gomchen, who did not resemble this one in the least. But he had a severe message for her. He told her that she did not carry well her disguise of poverty and that she had adopted the mentality of her incognito. She was more courageous when she wore her religious mantle and her rosary around her neck. He advised her to don the robe and rosary once she had left Lhasa, which she would surely reach.[15]

After four months of traveling over diverse terrain they saw the golden roofs of the Potala gleaming before them. Their arrival was signaled by a sudden tempest that sent sand swirling into the air, surrounding them with a concealing yellow veil. For this timely gesture they thanked the same benevolent genie who had protected them from so many dangers en route. As the storm subsided they were greeted by a kind woman who had noticed how very tired and travel-worn they were, and she volunteered to lead them to a place where they could rent a room. This was most fortunate, because the city was thronged with pilgrims who had arrived to participate in the festivities of the New Year. The room, situated in a half-ruined building, was very small, but possessed a magnificent view of the city and the Potala. Again their "genie" had provided. Within their room at last they felt it was safe to exclaim, "Lha gyalo! Di tamtchen pam!" ("The gods have triumphed! The demons have been vanquished!")

Their sojourn in Lhasa lasted two months, during which they sauntered through the streets, palaces, and temples, observing all the colorful and exotic spectacles of the Tibetan New Year's celebration. There was nothing of interest in the bazaars. The object most in view was an ordinary aluminum saucepan, such as one might find in any European hardware store, displayed in a variety of sizes. Of sanitary facilities there were none. Areas of

ground were set aside for this purpose. But the long
robes worn by both men and women served to conceal
their occupation so skillfully that an uninformed observer would think, seeing these groups of people seated,
that they were merely chatting.[16]

But as usual, the most entertaining spectacle was
provided by the two unknown "intruders" themselves.
They had decided that it might be more politic to examine the interior of the Potala in the company of others.
As they arrived before the entrance Yongden noticed two
male visitors from the provinces ogling the decor. They
would serve perfectly. Accosting them as though he were
a lama associated with the sacred edifice, he demanded
if they wouldn't like to have a guided tour of the interior.
No, not really. They had concluded the affair that had
brought them to the city and had other ideas about how
to enjoy the hours that were left. Oh, but how could they
pass up such a marvelous opportunity? One could always
get drunk, but only once in a lifetime could one visit the
interior of the Potala in company of a real expert! As
they were talking, he gradually led them through the
door. So mesmerized were they by the lama's rhetoric,
the "tour" had begun before they knew what had happened. But Alexandra was not so lucky. As she began to
follow them, the way was suddenly barred by a short, fat
monk who ordered her to remove her cherished bonnet.
One could never enter the sacred palace wearing such a
miserable object. This amounted to a disaster. Beneath
the protection of her bonnet, Alexandra's hair had
regained its normal color. Her Chinese ink had been
exhausted long since, and the yak tail would have dis-
graced a rat. Wrapped around her reddish-brown hair
it created a coiffure that could have competed with any
circus clown. Nevertheless, she did as she was told. When
Yongden saw her he almost fainted. The only way to
make her less noticeable was to create a distraction
himself. He at once launched into a discourse concerning
the artifacts in the Potala that would have amazed and

edified the Dalai Lama himself. Others joined the audience and listened with awe and admiration, commenting on the kindness of the erudite lama in taking so much trouble for simple, unlettered people. No one even noticed Alexandra's curious coiffure. When at last the tour had been completed the grateful visitors offered the lama a most generous contribution for his time and trouble. It was an afternoon they would always remember. So would their guide and his mother.

As a city she did not find Lhasa particularly beautiful. The architecture expressed more opulence and power than grace, in her opinion. There were other sites in Tibet that she found more to her taste. But she never regretted having made the effort to visit the "forbidden city." Nevertheless, in her first letter to Phillipe after she had arrived, she avowed that even if she were offered a million to repeat the adventure under the same conditions, she would refuse."[17]

Arrivals are often anticlimactic. Later, however, she believed that she had succeeded as completely as the most demanding could dream, a picturesque voyage the qualities of which far surpassed those invented by Jules Verne, traversing regions never before visited by a European.[18]

Alexandra often declared how very much she regretted not having ended her life in the vastness of the Himalayan wilderness. Instead, her karma required that she live another forty-five years before her ashes dissolved in the Ganges and she merged at last with the land she so loved. But in spirit, she remained always on the heights, and in her eyes shone the eternal light of Tibet.

Epilogue

On May 10, 1925, Alexandra and Yongden returned to France in triumph. They were already celebrities. But the transition that followed was the greatest challenge she had yet faced. Long before she left Asia, her letters to Mouchy indicated that she was well aware of the reality of what life in France had become and was therefore most reluctant to return. He had assumed for a long time that she would remain in Asia, in India perhaps, or Indochina. She might well have established herself there. Numerous offers were made to supply her with a permanent dwelling and the opportunity to continue her research. The truth was that she wanted very much to see her husband again. But what she discovered on her return required a far more difficult adjustment than she had imagined. She was forced to confront all the sad bitterness and confusion of a France impoverished by years of war. She encountered a husband who, though willing to have supported her Asian "folie," refused to accept her with an adopted son and jealously resented Yongden's presence in her life. And there were the incessant demands of journalists and publishers who wished to capitalize on her as an "original" personality before someone else arrived on center stage.

There were few who understood the true motivation of her travels. Every voyager is concerned with some objective, a reason or at least a pretext given for his travels. One may be a geographer, another a naturalist. Alexandra's motivation was to gather manifestations of human thought, to attempt to penetrate the mystery of the world and ease man's fear of suffering and death.[1]

Neither the intellectual community nor the public in postwar France had any interest in such "interior" exploration. She had taken on the responsibility of a son. Now she was obliged to support them both with her pen. Had she been a man, any number of universities would have offered her a professor's chair and undertaken to support her research in oriental studies. Instead she was forced to undertake a long series of popular literary undertakings in order merely to survive. The public adored her recitals of adventure, of the magic and mystery of esoteric rites, and her colorful descriptions of exotic places to which they could journey comfortably in an armchair. Her lectures in Paris, London, Brussels, and Geneva were packed. She had an enormous and enthusiastic following, which included the president of France and the queen of Belgium. After her first volume, *Voyage d'une Parisienne à Lhassa*, appeared, the demand for sequels never abated. When she died at the age of a hundred and one she left four major works in progress. But the research that had really motivated her travels she was never able to complete. There were those in academic circles who were even cruel enough to chide her for depreciating her knowledge to please the public. And she was severely criticized by many who knew little of the facts for taking advantage of her "poor husband." To this day, when freedom of behavior is taken quite for granted, it is her conduct that arouses the greatest interest. Did she really lie on a bed of nails? Of course it is obvious that she was the maharajah's mistress! And her guru? He must have hypnotized her! As for her dream of Buddhist reform, it remained forever buried in the snows of the Himalayan mountains.

After she and Yongden established themselves at Digne, in the Alps of Provence, where the climate suited her always-fragile health, they worked constantly, day and night, even selling the produce they grew on their land in order to survive. The French government was eager for her to return to Asia, however, and efforts were made to arrange for the necessary subsidies. Finally, after long negotiations and years of preparation, the project materialized. Aided by a substantial grant, she and Yongden returned to China by way of the Siberian railway across Russia in 1937. She planned to research various remote branches of Buddhism in outlying areas, such as Siberia and outer Mongolia, as well as to produce a Tibetan grammar. Although in principle she had supported the revolution in Russia, and anticipated a warm welcome for one who wished to observe the improved conditions in that country, the reality was a great disappointment. Her visit was brief and carefully monitored. What little she was able to observe at close hand disillusioned her about the Bolsheviks. Once again the timing was disastrous. Soon after she arrived in China, war was unleashed both in Asia and in Europe, making her return impossible. After repeated efforts to escape the increasing horrors of the Sino-Japanese war, she took refuge in Tatsienlu in southeastern Tibet and remained in this dreary, uninspiring outpost until March 1944, when she was able to move on to Chengtu. She left China on the verge of civil war to return to an India already in the throes of revolution. In spite of all this upheaval and turmoil she still hoped to remain in Asia for the remainder of her life. But in the interval her "bien cher Mouchy" had died and she was forced to return to Europe to settle his estate.

Her love for Mouchy had only increased with the years. She constantly begged him to visit her in Digne, and tried her best to convince him that the presence of the devoted Yongden could, in fact, render his old age more agreeable. She concerned herself with all the details of his life, implored him to spend more time with her, and frequently offered him money as her financial situation improved. Finally, as his life was drawing to a close there are indications from his letters that her deep affection was returned. The many years of separation and misunderstanding were resolved in the "belle histoire d'amour" of two elderly intransigents. Her response to the telegram that informed her of his death was simply to comment sadly that she had lost a wonderful husband and her only friend."[2]

Her second return, in 1946, was even more triumphal than the first. The books that resulted from this journey[3] found a continuing and enthusiastic audience, and were translated into many languages. The demand for her as a lecturer and "mentor" of Buddhist societies was so great it became too much to fulfill, and she returned to Digne to find some well-deserved rest. There she rebuilt her home, damaged during the war, and even allowed herself the luxury of an automobile, which Yongden delighted in chauffeuring. In the Digne archives there are marvelous photos (her enthusiasm for photography continued unabated), of the two rotund, well-turned-out tourists en voyage—an amusing postscript to their prodigious adventures. Her home was visited by a long series of admirers, such as Queen Elizabeth of Belgium, with whom she corresponded regularly, Princess Marie Bonaparte, and Prince Pierre of Greece. The visiting cards, many of them crested, numbered in the hundreds. Yongden thoroughly enjoyed the pleasures of Digne, which had become an important mountain resort with baths and cultural activities. Small and round, wearing a rakish Basque beret, he was a favorite personality in the city, where he was occasionally tempted into a café for a glass of beer and a cigarette, against the strict prohibition of his mother, who thought of him always as an adolescent. Their lives resumed a tranquil rhythm of activity, of study, meditation, translation of Buddhist texts, and gardening, which was a favorite diversion.

In the middle of an October night in 1955 Alexandra was aroused by a frantic knocking on her door. In her half-awakened state she recalled the Tibetan superstition that death knocks thus seeking entrance, and she refused to answer. The pounding became more insistent.

"Monsieur is very ill!" The physician who was summoned at once could do nothing. In a few hours Yongden was dead of severe uremic poisoning.

She who, with stoic equanimity, had always prided herself on looking life and death squarely in the face, was overwhelmed by a grief that nothing could assuage. For hours, in deepest mourning, she sat motionless before the urn that contained his ashes. She did not write, she did not work, she longed only to join him in death. Inconsolable, she was haunted by the memory of the lamentations of the Chinese innkeeper who had cried out in vain beside her dying son.

But gradually, very gradually, she began to resume her life. Her small body, though severely crippled by arthritis, refused to give in. In 1959 she had the good fortune to employ a sympathetic, intelligent young woman as companion and secretary. With the help of Marie-Madeleine Peyronnet, whom she affectionately christened "Tortue" (turtle), she once again immersed herself in her translations and writing. Marie-Ma was the constant companion of her last ten years, years that were filled with activity and honors. She was made a *commandeur* of the Légion d'honneur, and a coin of the French mint was issued in her honor. Although she wanted no ceremony on the occasion of her one hundredth birthday, she ended up participating enthusiastically in all the activities of the long day, enjoying every minute of it. She decided to have her passport renewed "just in case." It was prophetic. Provided as always with the necessary document, she departed on her last and greatest adventure.

A question I am frequently asked by those who are interested in the life of Alexandra is: "Did all of her years of effort and searching bring her peace of mind? Did she in fact achieve enlightenment?" It is a question Alexandra herself would have hesitated to answer. The most candid revelations of her inner life she shared only with Mouchy, and these ended abruptly with his death in 1941. It is certain that her devotion to Buddhism never flagged. Buddhism is, above all, a way of life, a path to be followed, not a subject for speculation or philosophic observation. And it is clear that she walked that path to the very end of her life, never deviating from her allegiance to its principles of tolerance, compassion, and open, objective investigation. All of her ideas, opinions, and sentiments were questioned and rigorously examined before being accepted. Her delight in the exploration of meaning never ceased. Marie-Ma recounts that she would devote days to researching the precise word that would convey her intention.

What, then, was her spiritual achievement? This word "spiritual" applied to Buddhism sometimes produces confusion and misunderstanding. In a dualistic Christian context it implies that which is the opposite of physical or material: heaven as oppposed to earth. A spiritual person is seen as one capable of transcending everyday, mundane reality, one who exists on a "higher" level of consciousness, whose goals and intentions are antimaterialistic. This model has in part also imposed chastity, sobriety, and seriousness as opposed to sexuality and the acceptance of earthly pleasures and human frailty. The goal of the Buddhist is rather not an escape from, but an engagement with, the life of this world. The image most frequently employed is that of a path or a way; one that leads the follower out of the suffering of existence, the suffering inherent in sickness, aging, deterioration, and death, as experienced by all living creatures. Alexandra often emphasized that the "high walls" of the Judeo-Christian ethic that shelter the monastic vocation in the West were unnecessary protection for one who trod the Buddhist Path. The requirements were rather a willingness to face life squarely and to seek truth with diligence, good humor, and, above all, an open mind.

Terms such as "enlightenment" and "satori" imply

that the way out of suffering can be achieved once and for all in a kind of "Big Bang" illumination that installs one definitively above and beyond mundane realities. As identified by Alexandra in the context of her own experience, the Way is comparable to a composition once described by a music critic as "a sequence of sublime moments separated by interminable half hours."[4] Both during and after her lifetime she was a source of speculation. Was she truly a sorceress? Did she engage in mysterious tantric sexual rites? Could she leave her body and travel on the astral plane?—et cetera, et cetera, ad absurdum. What can be said without exaggeration is that Alexandra fulfilled her days with dedication and unflagging purpose. She surmounted painful physical limitations, illness, much sadness and disappointment. Her concern was less with "spirituality" than with survival. She confronted the prospect of death with a calm equanimity. She prevailed over all the vicissitudes that blocked her way.

Not long before the end of her life Alexandra was questioned by Marie-Ma about what she felt she had accumulated in the way of understanding. She replied that in truth she knew nothing at all and was only beginning to learn.[5] What greater accomplishment could there be for a devout Buddhist than to have retained beginner's mind after one hundred years?

The great auditorium in Digne was suddenly silent. Respectfully the capacity crowd rose, hands pressed together, to greet a slender, smiling man wearing the garnet toga of a Buddhist monk. Accompanied by a prestigious following of lamas gathered from throughout the Western world, His Holiness, Tenzin Gyatso, the fourteenth Dalai Lama, had returned to Digne. His teaching was a model of simplicity, an exposition of the purest, most ancient and universal truths of the Dharma, the Buddhism of Buddha as Alexandra had believed it should be. She had endured many long years of disappointment and frustration, feeling that her true vocation had been abandoned. Yet her unflagging effort unquestionably helped to pave the way for the Buddhism that has attracted increasing numbers of adherents in Europe and America. As the Dalai Lama formulated his tribute to her, I could not resist a smiling reflection: Alexandra, your "magic" is still very much alive. Your beloved Tibet has come West at last, to you.

Appendix
The Buddhist Writings

Le Bouddhisme du Bouddha, by Alexandra David-Néel, was first published in 1911. The present edition is handsomely presented by the Editions du Rocher of Monte Carlo. A revised and abridged version appeared briefly in England in 1939, was subsequently a "casualty of the war," and reappeared in 1977 with a forward by Alexandra's good friend Christmas Humphreys.

What is remarkable about the original French edition is that Alexandra managed to present such a complete, scholarly, and readable work at a period of her life when she was suffering a serious physical and emotional crisis. Her marriage to Philippe Néel was on the verge of dissolution, her health was weakened by a combination of psychosomatic illnesses, neurasthenia (as depression and nervous tension were then called), and digestive disorders. She was constantly traveling between North Africa, Paris, and London, writing articles for magazines and journals, on trains and boats, and in hotel rooms, lecturing and participating in meetings and conferences on every subject from religion to education, to women's suffrage. That in the midst of this turmoil she found the time and energy to produce such a splendid work is truly remarkable. It also reveals how deep was her understanding of Hindu and Buddhist thought even before she left for her long pilgrimage to the Orient. It is sad that such an erudite presentation would later be effaced by her more autobiographic "adventure stories," which had such popular appeal.

The book is of interest not only for its concise description of Buddhist teachings of all the major traditions, including the modern reforms, but also for its revelation of Alexandra's intellectual heritage, that of the cultured European of her time. She brought to her task the classically oriented education of the nineteenth century combined with an early-twentieth-century confidence in scientific progress. In evidence also are the strong tradition of French Protestantism and a conviction of the perfectibility of man, which fueled her enthusiasm for reform. She possessed a socialist desire for equality, a stoic suspicion of excess, and an always aristocratic aesthetic. It must be remembered that her conversion to Buddhism took place in a museum among the great treasures of Asiatic art.

Her knowledge of Sanskrit is clearly evident throughout the volume. She had studied the texts not only in French and English translations, but in the original Sanskrit versions. She possessed an extraordinary facility for languages. How else could she have learned the multitude of dialects that served to protect her disguise on the route to Lhasa?

Alexandra did not come empty to Buddhism. She carried with her all her previous karmic baggage of tastes, prejudices, fantasies, and desires. She could easily have contented herself with a Theosophic approach or joined one of the esoteric groups available in Paris. Instead, she plunged into the essence of Buddhist thought by developing her expertise in language. She accepted nothing on faith, but was determined, in the purest Buddhist tradition, to explore, examine, and test the teaching for herself. This path she followed with rigor and perseverance to the very end of her life.

In her introduction she criticizes the emphasis on the classical Greek and Roman tradition in the popular education of the day, and the complete ignorance of the rich cultural heritage of the Aryan Indian civilization. She also deplores what she refers to as the "fantastic"

literature of Theosophy, occultism, and spiritism popular in Paris at that time. It must be emphasized, however,
that she treated the Theosophists, both in London and
Paris, with friendly respect, and through her frequent
lectures she encouraged them to deepen their understanding of the original texts. Her interest in and famil-
iarity with the discoveries of current scientific investigation is evident throughout the work, and she makes
frequent comparisons between the ancient tradition and
modern scientific concepts of the composition of the
universe. The area in which she reveals a certain weakness is that of the psychoanalytic theories of Freud and
the French researchers, which must have circulated
among the intelligentsia of London and Paris. It is understandable that she was hesitant to explore this area
in depth, in view of her very real personal dilemmas at
the time. She may have been wary of something that
touched her personal life. Her later commentary indi-
cates that she more than made up for this lack of
interest, that she became very much aware of the research being carried out on the influence of the subconscious mind on behavior.

Buddhism's lack of emotional appeal and its avoidance
of "religiosity" found favor with Alexandra's stoic agnosticism, and the emphasis on each individual's struggle
against suffering paralleled her own experience, even in
childhood, as a "loner." It is possible that this master
work was precipitated by the loss of her father—the only
individual with whom she had had any close human
contact. The book may have represented a catharsis
necessary for her to move on to a new life. *Le Bouddhisme du Bouddha* was a door through which Alexandra moved from one mode of investigation to another—
from scholarly research to individual experience. As
such it is seminal in the development of her thought. The
book preceded her to Japan, where it ensured her an
enthusiastic welcome and opened the doors of the Zen

tradition. In the midst of the Chinese revolution she was asked to produce a Chinese translation.

The way in which she compares the Buddhist and Christian traditions is interesting. She comments, when writing of the fact that the highest Buddhist teaching is reserved for an intellectual elite, that the "popularization" of Christianity in the early centuries A.D. resulted in the "paganizing" of the original faith. She was well versed in the Christian scriptures, having assiduously studied the Old and New Testaments from the time she could read. During her years in North Africa she had become acquainted with the Moslem tradition as well.

A theme that would recur is mentioned in the introduction: her disapproval, even despair, because of the veils of superstition that had been added to the original "pure" doctrine during ensuing centuries. And she had as yet to witness the extent to which this was true in Sikkim and Tibet. But beyond the "shabby religiosity of these sad disciples of the great Indian sage" there were two glorious ideas that served to overcome her repugnance: an absolute tolerance that is never denied, and the notion of salvation through understanding and intelligence alone.[1]

The first chapter is a detailed, poetic account of the life of the Buddha, which Alexandra postulates as legend rather than historical fact. She cites the writings of the French orientalists P. Foucher, of the Sorbonne, and Sylvian Lévi of the Collège de France, with whom she had studied, as well as Oldenberg, Rhys Davids, and a number of Sanskrit texts.

In the second chapter she examines the Four Truths: Suffering, the Cause of Suffering, the Desire to Overcome Suffering, and the Way out of Suffering, continually emphasizing determinism. Buddhism represents a method by means of which one may achieve one's own salvation. She refers to the Vedantic texts and reveals an extraordinary understanding of the literature and the influence of Hindu thought on Buddhism. Her scholarly precision is impeccable. She cites many writers: P. Lakshmi Narusa, Max Müller, Maung Nee, Nyanatiloka, Rhys Davids, H. Dharmapala, Ananda Mitraya, and M. Karoda. She refers often to the experimental, scientific approach of the "modern" Buddhists, with whose program of reform she had already identified.

It is interesting to follow the course of her thinking about reincarnation. In the beginning she lumps this belief with other "childish superstitions." At a later time, after she had devoted years to study and meditation she admitted having memories of previous lives. It was difficult for her pragmatic, Western scientific self to accept this possibility, and she wavered back and forth between denial and acceptance.

The end of the chapter concerning the Four Truths is a long translation from the *Dhammapada* that gathers together the strands of her lengthy exposition. She preferred always to go directly to the oldest available sources, rather than to later commentaries of opinions.

In the chapter on meditation she explains the difference between meditation and prayer, and quotes extensively from Ananda Maitriya's *On the Culture of the Mind* and the *Mahasudassana Sutra*. The importance of establishing a regular routine in the practice of meditation is emphasized and various techniques and practices are described in detail. She explains the meaning of samadhi and how it is often misinterpreted in the West, emphasizing that meditation is a means to an end, a means of mental discipline, a source of awakening and understanding, and not an end in itself. Experiences of "ecstasy," according to Alexandra, do not contribute to enlightenment. She cites the "calm reflection" described by Nyanatiloka in his work *The Word of the Buddha*.[2]

The chapter on karma includes many references to the influence of Hindu thought and comparisons with Judeo-Christian concepts of the "will of God" and "free will." She states that suffering cannot be explained solely by the action of karma, citing at length the *Questions of*

King Milinda.[3] The concept of karma as "moral retribution," often popularly expressed, has absolutely no
basis in a philosophy that denies the existence of an
unchanging individual ego. Writing of the constant struggle between the tenacious human need for individual
justice and the Buddhist theory of impermanence and
nonpersonality, she repeats the question (posed by King
Milinda and many others): what is it that suffers the
results of karma and transmigrates from life to life? The
answer given by Narusa was that in the context of
Buddhism transmigration is simply a manifestation of
cause and effect. It is only by virtue of causes and
conditions that mental phenomena accompanied by bod-
ily forms are produced, and the character of the succession of lives that result is determined by the quality of
the mental phenomena.[4]

There remains a certain ambiguity, however, which
each seeker must resolve through personal experience.

The metaphor with which Alexandra concludes her
explanation of karma is that of a man who awakens in
the night, lights a lamp and, calling his secretary, dic-
tates a letter. The secretary then departs, the light is
extinguished, and the man goes back to sleep. All is as
before. But the letter remains—the persistence of the
accomplished act that will move on to produce other
actions. This is a parable of life in which activity is
engendered and then disappears, leaving behind the
result of its activity.[5] Alexandra admits that the popular
image of reincarnation reveals the profound reality that
a child who is born is not a newcomer but an actor
returning on scene to continue his or her role.[6]

The chapter on nirvana is primarily an effort to
clarify what is very much misunderstood by the Western
mentality. It has nothing whatever to do with death, but
represents a state of mind achieved by a living person.
"Instead of the blind faith usually required by other
religions, Buddhism demands of its followers the peace-
ful acceptance of uncertainty before the problems that

surpass the understanding of the spirit. . . . If we wish to understand what nirvana is, we must learn by our own experimentation, because nirvana by its very nature surpasses all definition."[7]

There are meaningful quotations from many scriptures concerning nirvana, emphasizing that the "extinction" signified by nirvana is the extinction of our attachment to individual existence. "The 'flame' which we must 'blow out' is the illusion of the ego. . . ."[8]

There is a brief chapter on the manner in which "Sangha" has changed in meaning from an actual religious community of monks or nuns to isolated individual seekers who remain in the world to fulfill their destinies as Buddhists, the communion of all those who bring together their common compassion for the misery of human beings and who vow to struggle against suffering and ignorance.[9]

In the final chapter she considers two problems "contemporary" at the time, the position of women in reference to Buddhism, and the question of "social action," in which she compares her socialist theories to Buddhist concepts. These were apparently no longer considered "contemporary" in 1939, because that chapter was omitted from the English version. In an extensive appendix she gives translations of many of her favorite texts.

Even today, after so many excellent books on Buddhism have appeared in the West, this volume can be recommended for its content, its form, and its organization. It is a pleasure to read, and the choice of texts is excellent.

The English version is a translation by Bernard Miall and H. N. M. Hardy of a revision published by Plon in 1936 under the title *Le Bouddhisme: ses doctrines et ses methodes*. The 1977 Unwin paperback edition has a foreword by her friend Christmas Humphreys. She had experienced Buddhism at first hand in various countries and cultures. Those elements of the teaching most important for one being introduced to Buddhism are emphasized. Although an adept of the Mahayana tradition, she gives an excellent explanation of the Theravada point of view. In the section on karma she offers her own elucidation of the *Bardo thod dol (Book of the Dead)*, which had just been presented to the West by W. Y. Evans-Wentz and Dawasandup, her old friend and interpreter, the "schoolmaster" of Sikkim.

In her introduction to the 1939 edition, she presents her work as part of an "inventory" of the intellectual capital possessed by humanity confronted by an imminent disaster. She emphasizes that she does not suggest "copying" or even seeking precise directions from the ancient masters. To do so only results in caricature. But she feels it is important to examine the fundamental precepts and the disciplines of the masters in order to better understand ourselves. She mentions the fact that this work is the fruit of a long collaboration with her son, Yongden. Christmas Humphreys comments that this very erudite work was not well received because her readers expected another even more titillating work on the mysteries of Tibet and were disappointed. It is also possible that dedicated seekers have been somewhat turned off by the popular works and tend not to take her Buddhist writings seriously. During the last twenty-five years I have devoted much time to reading books that are concerned with Buddhist teaching, and have pretty well covered the subject both in French and English. I always find something new and stimulating in the Buddhist literature of Alexandra David-Néel. Her work combines an exacting and meticulous scholarship with the enthusiasm of a committed seeker. The English version suffers somewhat from being too much abridged and from translation, which denies the reader the rich variety of her language.

Les Enseignements secrets des bouddhistes tibetains is one of the last works published before her death. It appeared in 1951. This small volume is the distilled essence of all that Alexandra had learned from her

Dharma masters over a period of twenty years. She was eighty-three years old when she completed it. It represents not only her teaching, but the many years of study, reflection, and collaboration with Yongden after their return to France. It is a volume to treasure, to be read and reread. In the first chapter, "The Secret," she explains that this "secret" refers not to the attitude of the teacher, but to the intellectual limitations of the student. Until the latter attains the level of understanding required to appreciate the teaching, it remains "secret," that is, unavailable. In Tibet it was assumed that such understanding could be achieved only after many lifetimes of study and concentration. There is absolutely no suggestion of supernatural influence in the transmission. It is the fruit of a long progression of experiences passed on through oral transmission from teacher to student. For the student the procedure involves infrequent interviews with the master, followed by long intervals of study, concentration, meditation, and reflection on the topic under consideration. When the student has thoroughly integrated this information, he is introduced to the next topic. Very gradually the teaching is assimilated as a living entity. What the teacher passes on to the student is not "information" but the capacity to learn for himself through experience.

The second chapter is "Seeing." First of all the student is encouraged to doubt. Only doubt incites the research required for complete understanding. And the most important objects of doubt are our own perceptions. The student is taught to examine all his perceptions and to understand the multiple influences of memory and reasoning that alter perception. We inhabit two worlds, one of pure contact, and one of interpretation. This second world, though quite "real," is totally illusory. The world of sensation consists only of movement—the incessant movement of separated sequences of events, the rapidity of which makes them seem continuous.

This leads to the conclusion that each of us, through his isolated interpretations of sensations, creates a personal reality that is independent and arbitrary. It is not a question of there existing a universe "in which" contact and sensation take place. These contacts and their effects are the universe. The dimension of time is also introduced. We see only what has transpired in the past. Our images are of phenomena that no longer exist (as in the example of the star we see sparkling in the sky, which ceased to exist billions of years ago).

The theory of the probability of future experience as understood by quantum research is also presented, using the well-known Zen metaphor of the bridge over a moving river. Does the river flow under the bridge, or do the observer and the bridge "progress" along a stationary body of water? The truth is that all these theories and doctrines are fabrications that result from the illusion experienced by our minds.

This is further elaborated in the chapter on the interdependent origins. Alexandra has produced a chart listing these origins in sequence, with the Sanskrit and Tibetan translations of each word. Again there is evoked the image of experience as a sequence of disconnected moving particles, like a long progression of ants approaching an ant hill. "Everything which exists, exists in dependence on a cause."[10]

We are these chains, which we have created in our state of ignorance, believing them to have a reality they do not possess. Her interest in and knowledge of psychoanalytic theory is revealed in this context. She states that the most powerful causes are those arising from the subconscious mind. And, invoking the energy emitted even by a blade of grass or a grain of sand, she echoes the poetic imagery of William Blake—certainly a kindred spirit. The process of observation alters our perception and serves to enhance the illusion that results when we make an effort to "examine" our environment.

Throughout her exposition she refers to original texts

and explains the Sanskrit and Tibetan orthography. She emphasizes that to read, examine, or even hear the ideas at length is insufficient for understanding. They must be integrated into one's own day-to-day experience.

The chapter on the Way is introduced by a long discussion on the meaning of the doctrine of *prajña paramita*, to which she later devoted an entire volume, *La Connaissance transcendante*, published in 1958. The Sanskrit meaning is translated as "excellent wisdom" or "highest understanding." The Tibetan and Chinese interpretation is to "pass beyond," to "go to the opposite bank." The difference in meaning is subtle, but very important. There is a popular belief that by means of leading a virtuous life one will achieve a happy reincarnation. But the second interpretation implies going beyond the practice of virtue to a condition where it becomes completely automatic—a reflex (such as withdrawing one's hand from a burning coal). This interpretation also implies passing beyond the very perception of virtue and vice and of all the other opposites, to an understanding and acceptance of the relativity of all phenomena. Even the concept of a goal—of attaining the "other bank"—ceases to exist. The famous "raft" that must be abandoned once one has reached the other bank of the river is referred to as being nothing more than an instrument. The "other shore" is situated neither in space nor in time. There is only the infinite "beyond" of unfolding experience. "The country that is in fact 'nowhere' is your true home."[11]

To have accepted this is to be fully liberated, to have attained a condition of "nonactivity," to have dropped the chains of enslavement, the "chain of gold" (the practice of virtue) as well as the "chain of iron" (the practice of vice), both of which are forged by the mental activity born of illusion. "It is enough to allow existence to flow, contemplating it as an interested and at times amused spectator, completely detached while being also aware that one is part of the spectacle, immersed in the flow, and moving with it."[12]

To have achieved this understanding is to have achieved nirvana. There are two possible routes, according to tradition: the gradual, a long process involving the practice of many virtues, and the direct. The latter can result from the slightest sight or sound that may occur at the moment when one is ready to leap into the unknown and see reality unveiled. But nirvana, believed by many to represent the opposite of samsara (the world of illusion), is, according to the secret teaching, merely the same thing seen from another aspect.

A fascinating blend of psychoanalytic theory with reincarnation is her description of each individual as a "cluster" or "crowd of others," combining the multitude of past influences one has encountered in a lifetime. We are the "present incarnation" of these multiple clusters (influences) of previous lives reaching "back" in time and "out" in space. These "others" assume the form of fragmented tendencies that operate in the context of our present existence, now one, now another having a greater or lesser influence on our behavior. Alexandra reveals an excellent understanding of this theory of multiple forces reincarnated and reintegrated in the metaphor she creates of "life as theater," which she had herself experienced. "To believe that one knows is the greatest obstacle to wisdom."[13] The secret teaching encourages the student to continue always along the route of discovery.

"I never pretended to teach you anything. I only invited you to consider, to doubt, and to seek."[14]

Notes

Introduction

1. Decaux, Alain, *Histoire des Françaises, II, La Révolte* (Librairie Academique Perrin, 1979), 919.
2. Ibid., 952.
3. Ibid., 962.
4. Ibid., 967.
5. For the history of English Buddhism I am indebted to a number of works by Christmas Humphreys, including *Buddhism* (New York: Penguin, 1951) and *Exploring Buddhism* (London: Unwin, 1974).
6. Quotation from the *Mahā-parinibbāna-sutta*.
7. A favorite anecdote of Mlle. Peyronnet, communicated to the author.

Chapter 1: A Small Anarchist

1. The incidents included in this chapter concerning the youth of Alexandra David-Néel were recounted orally by her to Marie-Madeleine Peyronnet during their ten years together. It is the latter who recounted them to the author. Alexandra retained an astonishing ability to recall details to the very end of her life. She was also, however, an accomplished storyteller, and one must take this into consideration, allowing her a certain "poetic license" in the presentation of her early adventures.
2. David-Néel, Alexandra, *Journal de voyage* (Paris: Plon, 1975), vol. 1, 20.
3. Ibid., 232–233.
4. Ibid., 207.
5. David-Néel, Alexandra, *Le Sortilège du mystère* (Paris: Plon, 1972). This anecdote is elaborated on pages 16–17.
6. Ibid., 14.

Chapter 2: En Route

1. David-Néel, *Le Sortilège*, 26.
2. Ibid., 13.
3. Ibid., 64–65.
4. Ibid., 65.
5. Ibid., 79.
6. Ibid., 85.
7. Ibid., 86.
8. Ibid., 86–87.
9. David-Néel, Alexandra, *L'Inde où j'ai vécu* (Paris: Plon, 1951), 12.
10. Ibid., 13.
11. Ibid., 17. Alexandra changed this to *tire-tire* (pull-pull).
12. Ibid., 18–19.
13. Ibid., 22.
14. Ibid., 322.
15. Ibid., 324.

Chapter 3: Beside the Other Life

1. Myrial, Alexandra, *Le Grand Art—journal d'une actrice*, unpublished ms., Digne Archives, 1902, 68.
2. Ibid., 130.
3. Ibid., 516–517.
4. Chalon, Jean, *Le Lumineux Destin d'Alexandra David-Néel* (Paris: Plon, 1985), 101ff.
5. Ibid., 519.
6. Recounted by Marie-Madeleine Peyronnet to the author.

Chapter 4: Philippe

1. Louis David to Philippe Néel, July 1904, Digne Archives.
2. A few notes from Alexandra's diary of 1900 (Digne Archives). "February 14—Project for a book: *The Modern Saints*; February 15—Write to DeRosny for the Congress of Ethnology; February 17—Title for book: *Women in Love and Marriage*; March 7—Notes on Catholic processions in Spain and Pays Basque; June 28—Research for voyage to Tunis; July 7—Dined on the terrace of Carthage under a full moon."
3. David-Néel diary, 1900.

4. Ibid.
5. Decaux, *Histoire*, 963.
6. "Alouch" means sheep in Arabian. Alexandra thought he was as "curly as a sheep." She also referred to him as "Mouchy," diminutive for "Mamamouchi," another Arabian name.
7. Louis David to Alexandra David-Néel, July 5, 1904, Digne Archives.
8. David-Néel, *Journal*, vol. 1, 32.
9. David-Néel diary, 1904, Digne Archives.
10. Ibid., August 19, 1905.
11. Ibid., January 1906.
12. Ibid., January 1, 1907.
13. Ibid., January 15, 1907.
14. Ibid., January 22, 1910.
15. David-Néel, *Journal*, vol. 1, 22.
16. Alexandra David-Néel to Philippe Néel, Paris, September 27, 1904, Digne Archives.
17. Philippe Néel to Alexandra David-Néel, Tunis, 1907 (?), Digne Archives.
18. Alexandra David-Néel to Philippe Néel, Digne Archives.
19. Ibid., January 4, 1905.
20. David-Néel diary, Digne Archives.
21. Alexandra David-Néel to Philippe Néel, Digne Archives.

Chapter 5: The Search Begins

1. David-Néel, *Journal*, vol. 1, 56.
2. Ibid., 57.
3. Ibid., 58.
4. Ibid., 63.
5. Ibid., 60.
6. Ibid., 65–66.
7. Ibid., 67.
8. Alexandra David-Néel to Philippe Néel, Adyar-Madras, November 27, 1911, Digne Archives.
9. David-Néel, *Journal*, vol 1, 76.
10. Ibid., 79.
11. Ibid., 80.
12. David-Néel diary, January 1, 1912, Digne Archives.
13. David-Néel, *Journal*, vol. 1, 83.

14. Alexandra David-Néel to Philippe Néel, Calcutta, January 13, 1912, Digne Archives.

Chapter 6: Sikkim the Incomparable

1. David-Néel, *Journal*, vol. 1, 118.
2. Ibid., 119.
3. Ibid., 121.
4. Ibid., 123.
5. Ibid., 124–125.
6. The documents that resulted are now preserved in the archives at Digne.
7. David-Néel, *Journal*, vol. 1, 126–127. The struggle on the part of the Tibetans to expel the remnants of the invading Chinese had almost reached the frontier of Sikkim. The British administration did not wish to be held responsible for her safety under these conditions. During this period of delicate diplomatic negotiations among Russia, Great Britain, and China, all of whom desired the "protection" of Tibet as a buffer state, Tibet was effectively closed to outside exploration and influence. The Lhasa government desired to remain as remote as possible, and the British were trying valiantly to contain the influence of the Chinese, while, at the same time, allowing them to save face. The British efforts to prevent Alexandra from visiting Lhasa, however, evolved into a personal contest of wills. The British colonial administrators did not enjoy having their authority flaunted by "la Parisienne."
8. Ibid., 138.
9. Alexandra David-Néel to Philippe Néel, May 23, 1912, Digne Archives.
10. Ibid., May 28, 1912.
11. David-Néel, *L'Inde*, 211.
12. Ibid.
13. David-Néel, *Journal*, vol. 1, 179.
14. Ibid., 148.
15. Sidkeong Tulku to Alexandra David-Néel, September 8, 1912, Digne Archives.
16. David-Néel, *Journal*, vol. 1, 160–161.
17. Ibid., 161.
18. Ibid., 169.

19. Charles Bell, political officer in Sikkim, served as liaison between the Dalai Lama and the British government. There developed between the two men a warm friendship.
20. David-Néel, *Journal*, vol. 1, 172.
21. Ibid., 183.
22. Ibid., 188.
23. Alexandra David-Néel to Philippe Néel, October 5, 1912, Digne Archives.
24. David-Néel, *Journal*, vol. 1, 195.
25. Ibid., 187.

Chapter 7: Paradise Lost

1. This beautiful little image now resides in a place of honor on the altar in the Buddhist chapel at Samten Dzong. Alexandra had requested that it be returned to Sikkim after her death. Because of the political strife that was not possible. Marie-Ma Peyronnet has asked the Dalai Lama to take it with him to Tibet when at last he is able to return to his own country.
2. Alexandra David-Néel to Philippe Néel, November 23, 1912, Digne Archives.
3. Ibid., December 12, 1912.
4. David-Néel, *Journal*, vol. 1, 229.
5. *Samadhi*—a state of deep concentration with loss of awareness of the outside world.
6. *Sannyasin*—one who has renounced the world to become a wandering religious seeker.
7. Alexandra David-Néel to Philippe Néel, March 17, 1913, Digne Archives.
8. Ibid., March 17, 1913.
9. Ibid., April 1, 1913.
10. *Ghats*—terraces along Indian riverbanks.
11. David-Néel, *Journal*, vol. 1, 238.

Chapter 8: In the Ways of the Heart

1. Alexandra David-Néel to Philippe Néel, Gangtok, December 7, 1913, Digne Archives.
2. David-Néel, *Journal*, vol. 1, 260–261.
3. Marie-Ma Peyronnet says that it was when she was sedentary that Alexandra's numerous maladies became accentuated.

Once en route, or seriously occupied with a project, they miraculously disappeared.

4. Padmasambhava introduced tantric Buddhism into Tibet from India in the eighth century A.D..

5. David-Néel diary, January 13, 1914, Digne Archives.

6. David-Néel, *Journal*, vol. 1, 267.

7. Alexandra David-Néel to Philippe Néel, Gangtok, January 11, 1914, Digne Archives.

8. Ibid., May 5, 1914.

9. David-Néel, *Journal*, vol. 1, 281.

10. Ibid., 284.

11. Alexandra David-Néel to Philippe Néel, Gangtok, July 14, 1914, Digne Archives.

12. Ibid., July 6, 1914.

13. Ibid., August 24, 1914.

14. Ibid., August 10, 1914.

15. David-Néel, *Journal*, vol. 1, 306.

16. "It is finished. Life goes on." David-Néel, *Journal*, vol. 1, 308.

17. David-Néel diary, October 27, 1914, Digne Archives.

18. Alexandra David-Néel to Philippe Néel, De-Chen Ashram, May 2, 1915, Digne Archives.

19. David-Néel diary, September 26, 1912, Digne Archives.

20. Alexandra received many gifts. Marie-Ma Peyronnet commented on the large and devoted following she gathered and maintained during her long life, witnessed by the boxes of letters from all over the world contained in the archives in Digne. Her determination was equaled only by her intense loyalty and devotion to her friends.

21. David-Néel, *Journal*, vol. 1, 348–349.

22. Ibid.. 369.

23. Ibid., 382.

Chapter 9: The Miraculous Tree

1. David-Néel, *Journal*, vol. 1, 383.

2. Alexandra David-Néel to Philippe Néel, Darjeeling, September 17, 1916, Digne Archives.

3. *Le Bouddhisme du Bouddha* (Monaco: Editions du Rocher, 1977).

4. Daisetz Teitaro Suzuki, whose English-language texts introduced the principles of Zen Buddhism to the West.

5. David-Néel, *Journal*, vol. 1, 395.

6. Alexandra David-Néel to Philippe Néel, Kyoto, July 6, 1917, Digne Archives.

7. Ibid., April 8, 1917.

8. David-Néel, *Journal*, vol. 1, 424.

9. Ibid., 426.

10. Alexandra David-Néel to Philippe Néel, Peking, October 31, 1917, Digne Archives.

11. David-Néel, *Journal*, vol. 2, 17.

12. Ibid., 32.

13. Ibid., 38.

14. Ibid.

15. David-Néel, Alexandra, *Magic and Mystery in Tibet* (New York: Dover, 1971).

Chapter 10: The Eye of the Storm

1. David-Néel, *Journal*, vol. 2, 74.

2. The "great mule" had replaced Alexandra's beloved black mare. She was devoted to this animal and they played together like children.

3. David-Néel, *Journal*, vol. 2, 85.

4. Ibid., 92.

5. Ibid., 95.

6. Ibid., 96.

7. Alexandra David-Néel to Philippe Néel, September 18, 1920, Digne Archives.

8. David-Néel, *Journal*, vol. 2, 100.

9. Ibid., 121.

10. Ibid., 137.

Chapter 11: Where the Sky Is Blue

1. In 1945 Yongden was officially recognized as a "lama-tulku, lama-reincarnate" by the central government of China. He never used the title, however.

2. David-Néel, Alexandra, *Au pays des brigands gentilshommes* (Paris: Plon, 1980), 46.

3. Ibid., 23–24.

4. Ibid., 128.

5. Ibid., 164.
6. David-Néel, Alexandra, and Lama Yongden, *The Superhuman Life of Gesar of Ling* (Boston: Shambhala, 1987).
7. Alexandra David-Néel to Philippe Néel, Kanchow, January 1, 1923, Digne Archives.
8. Ibid.
9. Ibid., January 16, 1923.
10. David-Néel, *Journal*, vol. 2, 245.

Chapter 12: Footprints on the Wind

1. Kha Karpo—a chain of mountains situated in the northwest of Yunnan, China, that is a favorite place of pilgrimage for Tibetans.
2. David-Néel, Alexandra, *Voyage d'une Parisienne à Lhassa* (Paris: Plon, 1927), 28.
3. Ibid., 29.
4. The route suggested by Sir George Pereira, British geographer and explorer, whom David-Néel met in Jakyendo. See text, page 165.
5. David-Néel, *Voyage à Lhassa*, 39.
6. Ibid., 51.
7. Ibid., 94.
8. Chorten—a sacred monument to be found frequently along the routes in Tibet.
9. Bardo—the region "traversed" immediately after death, preceding reincarnation.
10. David-Néel, *Voyage à Lhassa*, 158.
11. Ibid., 178.
12. Ibid., 181.
13. Ibid., 184.
14. Ibid., 305.
15. Ibid., 310.
16. Ibid., 344.
17. David-Néel, *Journal*, vol. 2, 245.
18. Ibid., 251.

Epilogue

1. David-Néel, *Brigands gentilshommes*, 104.
2. David-Néel, *Journal*, vol. 2, 359.
3. *Sous les nuées d'orages* (Paris: Plon, 1940), *A l'ouest bar-*

bare de la vaste Chine (Paris: Plon, 1947), *Le Vieux Tibet face à la Chine nouvelle* (Paris: Plon, 1953).

4. The composition was *Parsifal* by Richard Wagner. The name of the critic I have unfortunately forgotten.

5. Personal communication to the author from Marie-Madeleine Peyronnet.

Appendix: The Buddhist Writings

1. David-Néel, *Le Bouddhisme du Bouddha*, 17.

2. Ibid., 161. Nyanatiloka is the religious name of a German Orientalist who lived more than forty years as a Buddhist monk in Ceylon. He wrote *Das Wort des Buddha* (The Word of the Buddha) and other translations. He died in 1947.

3. *The Questions of King Milinda* is a text popular with Hinayana Buddhists. Milinda was a historic personage who reigned over Bactria, to the east of India, after the time of the conquest by Alexander the Great, around 200 B.C. He was known also as Menander or Menandrosa. Alexandra David-Néel, *Buddhism, its Doctrines and its Methods* (London: Unwin Paperbacks, 1978), 174.

4. David-Néel, *Le Bouddhisme du Bouddha*, 183.

5. Ibid., 191.

6. Ibid., 193.

7. Ibid., 209.

8. Ibid., 222.

9. Ibid., 241.

10. David-Néel, Alexandra, *Les Enseignements secrets des bouddhistes tibétains* (Paris: Adyar, 1985), 54.

11. Ibid., 87.

12. Ibid., 95.

13. Ibid., 120.

14. Ibid.

Bibliography

Works by Alexandra David-Néel

A l'ouest barbare de la vaste Chine. Paris: Librairie Plon, 1947.

Astravakra Gita—Avadhuta Gita. 1958. Reprint. Monaco: Editions du Rocher, 1979.

Au coeur des Himalayas, le Népal. 1949. Reprint. Paris: Editions Pygmalion, 1978.

Au pays des brigands gentilshommes. 1933. Reprint. Paris: Librairie Plon, 1980.

Le Bouddhisme du Bouddha. 1936. Reprint. Monaco: Editions du Rocher, 1977.

En Chine. Paris: Librairie Plon, 1970.

La Connaissance transcendante. Paris: Librairie Adyar, 1958.

Les Enseignements secrets des bouddhistes tibétains. 1951. Reprint. Paris: Librairie Adyar, 1985.

Immortalité et réincarnation. 1961. Reprint. Monaco: Editions du Rocher, 1978.

L'Inde où j'ai vécu. 1951. Reprint. Paris: Librairie Plon, 1969.

Initiations lamaïques. Paris: Librairie Adyar, 1957.

Journal de voyage. 2 vols. Paris: Librairie Plon, 1975.

Le Lama aux cinq sagesses. With Lama Yongden. 1935. Reprint. Paris: Librairie Plon, 1977.

La Lampe de sagesse. Monaco: Editions du Rocher, 1986.

Magie d'amour et magie noire. 1940. Reprint. Paris: Librairie Plon, 1977.

Le Modernisme bouddhiste et le Bouddhisme du Bouddha. Librairie Félix Alcan, 1911. (Republished as Le Bouddhisme de Bouddha, Editions du Rocher, 1977.)

Mystiques et magiciens du Tibet. 1929. Reprint. Paris: Librairie Plon, 1968.

La Puissance du néant. 1954. Reprint. Paris: Librairie Plon, 1978.

Quarante siècles d'expansion chinoise. Paris: Libirairie Plon, 1964.

Le Sortilège du mystère. Paris: Librairie Plon, 1972.

Sous les nuées d'orages. 1940. Reprint. Paris: Librairie Plon, 1980.

Textes tibétains inédits. 1952. Reprint. Paris: Editions Pygmalion, 1978.

Le Tibet d'Alexandra David-Néel. Paris: Librairie Plon, 1979.

La Vie surhamaine de Guésar de Ling. Transl. Alexandra David-Néel
and Lama Yongden. 1931. Reprint. Monaco: Editions du Rocher,
1978.

Le Vieux Tibet face à la Chine nouvelle. 1953. Reprint. Paris, Librairie
Plon, 1981.

Vivre au Tibet. France, Editions Morel, (?).

Voyage d'une Parisienne à Lhassa. 1927. Reprint. Paris: Librairie Plon,
1983.

English Translations

Buddhism, Its Doctrines and Its Methods. New York: St. Martins's Press,
1978.

Initiations and Initiates in Tibet. Berkeley: Shambhala Publications,
1970.

Magic and Mystery in Tibet. 1932. Reprint. New York: Dover Publications, 1971.

My Journey to Lhasa. 1927. Reprint. Boston: Beacon Press, 1986.

The Power of Nothingness. Boston: Houghton Mifflin Co., 1982.

The Secret Oral Teachings in Tibetan Buddhist Sects. San Francisco:
City Lights Books, 1967.

The Superhuman Life of Gesar of Ling. Transl. Alexandra David-Néel
and Lama Yongden. 1934. Reprint. Boston: Shambhala Publications, 1987.

Biography

Chalon, Jean. *Le Lumineux destin d'Alexandra David-Néel.* Paris:
Librairie Plon, 1985.

Peyronnet, Marie-Madeleine. *Dix ans avec Alexandra David-Néel.* Paris:
Librairie Plon, 1973.